Advance
The Making of an Old Soul

Carol Orsborn's new book is a tour de force—heartfelt, honest, helpful, and healing.

—Andy Achenbaum, *Old Age in the New Land:*
The American Experience since 1790

Bursting with revelations, Carol's amazing book has set my mind spinning from insight overload! Healing and full of the fierce grace of enlightened aging, it may even help your grown children understand their parents' new and joyous weirdness. Dive in and discover the sacred mystery of your own life. This book will change you.

—John C. Robinson, *The Divine Human*

At 76 years old, I found this book to be a gift that I will treasure for as long as I live. It was the poet John Keats who spoke of our life as "the vale of soul-making." Alas, Keats knew nothing of old age, since he died at the age of 25. But his phrase is exactly what Carol Orsborn's book offers us: a passionate belief that later life can be a time of discovery, creation, and unfolding—becoming the person we were meant to be

—Harry (Rick) Moody, retired Vice President
for Academic Affairs, AARP

Carol Orsborn has written a stirring book to guide readers along a journey to "something more"— an intense, liberating spiritual merger with the divine. *The Making of an Old Soul* leads readers toward this final spiritual awakening, thus rewarding the struggles and lessons accumulated through a long life. This book wisely teaches why and how.

—Brent Green, *Questions of the Spirit: the Quest*
for Understanding at a Time of Loss

Carol Orsborn's book pulsates with the life and wisdom of an old soul. Through personal revelation, she encourages us to live our own lives hopefully, through both shadow and light, trusting that there is "something more" than we might see in the moment. Upon concluding her book, I wept, as I appreciated how remarkable this being human is. Carol and her book are gifts to the world, gifts that will gestate more life in us to be tasted and savored each day.

—Robert L. Weber, *The Spirituality of Age*

Praise for Carol Orsborn's
Writing on Aging and Spirituality

Carol Orsborn's contribution to the spirituality of age comes from deep research and even deeper personal experience. Her body of work includes the best book I have ever read on this most significant passage.

—Gail Sheehy, *Passages*

I savored *The Spirituality of Age* and commend this fine volume to anyone still searching, as I hope we all are, for the fullness of life.

—Harvey G. Cox, *The Future of Faith*

People across faith traditions as well as secularists will find *The Spirituality of Age* engaging and eye-opening

—Wade Clark Roof, *Spiritual Marketplace*

Spirituality of Age emphasizes that old age can be a time of growth and spiritual discovery, a time of fulfillment of life.

—Mary Catherine Bateson, *Composing a Further Life*

Carol Orsborn and Bob Weber have created a masterpiece! *The Spirituality of Age* is a must-read for all facing the quest for meaning and purpose in later life . . . I am buying copies for all my over-50 friends!

—Jane M. Thibault, *Pilgrimage into the Last Third of Life*

Fierce with Age is a thought-provoking, brave, and courageous look at aging. Carol Orsborn tackles both the shadow and the promise of transitioning to aging as the opportunity to grow whole, rather than just grow old.

—Ken and Maddy Dychtwald, co-founders of *Age Wave*

I've not read anything as honest and revealing as the tale of Carol Orsborn's personal journey into becoming *Fierce with Age*.

—Connie Goldman, *Who Am I . . . Now That I'm Not Who I Was*

I hope many people will follow the authors' lead in *Speak the Language of Healing* and learn something about their own souls in the process.

   —Harold S. Kushner, *When Bad Things Happen to Good People*

Speak the Language of Healing is an honest and heartfelt report . . . with a realization of the paradox: We are alone here, and yet at a profound level, we are not alone.

   —Jean Shinoda Bolen, *Close to the Bone*

The *Art of Resilience* is a wonderful new book about remembering the most important thing in life—love.

   —Gerald G. Jampolsky, *Love Is Letting Go of Fear*

The Making of an

OLD SOUL

The Making of an

OLD SOUL

Aging as the Fulfillment of Life's Promise

Carol Orsborn, Ph.D.

White River Press
Amherst, Massachusetts

First published 2021 by White River Press
Amherst, Massachusetts • whiteriverpress.com

ISBN: 978-1-935052-71-5 - paperback
          978-1-935052-76-0 - ebook

Book and cover design by Lufkin Graphic Designs
Norwich, Vermont • www.LufkinGraphics.com

Cover art:
"Afternoon Walk" by Susan Rios. Permission to use the cover painting in conjunction with this work is granted by Susan Rios. Sharing, duplication or dissemination in any way by written permission of the artist only. Susan Rios Designs www.susanriosdesigns.com and www.susanriosdesigns.etsy.com

Author's Note:
The sources for direct quotations are found in the bibliography. Variations of some of the entries in this book originally appeared in Carol Orsborn's blog *Older, Wiser, Fiercer* at CarolOrsborn.com and in previous editions drawn from her body of work. This is a work of nonfiction. In order to protect the privacy of individuals featured in the entries, some names, descriptions, and locations have been altered.

Library of Congress Cataloging-in-Publication Data:
Names: Orsborn, Carol, author.
Title: The making of an old soul : aging as the fulfillment of life's
    promise / Carol Orsborn.
Description: Amherst, Massachusetts : White River Press, 2021. | Includes
    bibliographical references.
Identifiers: LCCN 2021021558 | ISBN 9781935052715 (paperback)
Subjects: LCSH: Older people--Religious life. | Self-realization in old
    age. | Spiritual formation. | Aging--Psychological aspects. |
    Aging--Religious aspects.
Classification: LCC BL625.4 .O77 2021 | DDC 204/.40846--dc23
LC record available at https://lccn.loc.gov/2021021558

To Dan,
My Beshert

Contents

Prelude

W E WHO ARE GROWING OLD may well appear to have been diminished by time. But if you think so, you would be wrong. There are some amongst us not dulled but burnished by long lives, twists of fate, impossible choices, and grace into something most unexpected. We have not just become old. We have become old souls.

Burning with invisible passion and purpose, we live largely backstage in an alternate universe both wondrous and dangerous. We are at once inspired, beleaguered, and brave. This is the secret world of aging inhabited by the handful of hardy old souls who have found what we were looking for all our lives in the most unanticipated of times and places. What we discovered is nothing at all like what we'd anticipated but more than we'd hoped for. It is a state both small and humble and, at the same time, the peak of spiritual development. In this parallel universe, we gain access to the inner workings of the entire arc of life. At last, everything makes sense, and we come to understand that nothing of what we've been through from the moment we were conceived to the present was ever wasted. We have, in fact, burst through age to freedom.

The portal to this hidden dimension is hard to find under normal circumstances. Rather, it's a place that finds you, but only when you have given up trying to find it on your own. Do you have a sense of what I'm talking about? Do you persist in believing, despite the negative stereotypes of aging, that however old you are, there is enough time to get what you came here for? Then let this book affirm that your hope is merited and that you are a candidate for the fulfillment of life's promise. But be forewarned. It will take more than you've got, however in the end, you wouldn't have had it any other way.

— PART ONE —

The Portal Opens

AGING IN THE BEST OF TIMES is challenging. But growing old in an era when illusions of life mastery are not only eroded but shattered can also be a time of unexpected transformation. When aging coincides with a perilous period, there is an intensity that can break us free from the limitations of the past and into a future far more precious than we'd ever imagined for ourselves. But this unexpected transmutation is not a given. It comes most readily to those of us who have spent years in preparation and who willfully commit to using everything we've got. Still it takes something more.

I had just turned 72 in 2020 when I washed upon the desolate shore of the Covid-19 pandemic, something of a darkly hued psycho-spiritual come-as-you-are party for older people forced into extreme solitude by age and underlying conditions. We were caught in a moment of time in which we were exposed in all our vulnerability: isolated, undefended, and brought face-to-face with mortality before we were fully able to brace ourselves. I realize now that it is no accident that it would always have taken something as big as a global pandemic to break me out of the well-worn stories I'd been telling myself about my life, others, and the world over the years, foremost amongst them that the really bad things that happen to other people will never happen to me. At a time late in life I'd expected to be a culmination, I was instead confronted with a reckoning.

I was not alone. Devoid of diversion and support, those of us fortunate enough to take shelter with basic needs met had an abundance of time on our hands to dwell upon our litany of regrets, unanswered prayers, and questions of ultimate concern. During my year of sequester, I was just one among many grappling with a world where denial had broken open on so many levels. Whether doing my best to stay connected to family and friends or tuning into the nightly news, I did not know that I could shed so many tears, grieve so many losses, shudder with so much dread about the injustice in the world, not to mention confrontation with my own unintended contributions. Sweeping through it all was disappointment with the waves of fear about the all too real threat of the losses associated with age and mortality that routinely washed over me, having thought I'd made peace with death decades ago. Yet, here I was, after all these years of spiritual and psychological practice, feeling that I had been wrong about so many things.

It does not take a global crisis for age to disrupt the status quo. Age is completely capable of unsettling us on its own. Even before the pandemic, I awoke many mornings with a diffuse dread that the sense of arrival for which I yearned would somehow continue to elude me. While I believed myself to be at the peak of my knowledge and abilities, I was coming to realize that I was master of a universe that no longer exists. I often found myself brimming with unexpected passion, but frequently lacked the energy to see things through. At times I was full of purpose; other times I wondered what it had all been for. There were times I craved to be included while at the same time yearning for solitude: to be desperately wanted but desiring only to be left alone. I was fearful I wouldn't have enough courage and strength to meet the demands of the cavernous future that lay ahead, while also anxious that tomorrow could be my last. There was nothing serene, quiescent, or settled about any of this.

But not every new apprehension, even when unexpected, was unwanted. There were times, often when I was least expecting them, when I felt swept with indescribable peace and joy. There were moments—ephemeral though they may be—when, without doing anything other than feeling, I caught a whisper of truth that held the possibility of life's inherent meaning. I began to envision a time when, after years of productivity, I would no longer need to be the driven salmon in the river but the river itself: a force with which others must contend. These rare but precious moments of transcendence were experienced as a promise that forgives the past, cherishes the present, and welcomes the future, come what may. While the feeling of bliss both advanced and receded in my heart, I held onto the hope that a lifetime of debris could be carried away once and for all out to sea with the tide.

I encountered such a moment about two months into the pandemic of 2020, on a longer than usual walk through an old military cemetery near my home. I'd wandered among the rows and rows of starched white marble tombstones once before the pandemic, seeing only silent desolation. But this time was different. The day was just warming up enough to hint of summer to come, and for the first time I noticed that there were not only headstones but trees and flowers everywhere. Lavish sprays of deep purple lilacs incongruously draped over placard maps that separated the acres of tombstones into eras of conflict from the Civil War on. Cherry, ash, and willow were bursting loose in pulsating waves of green and vibrant splashes of color, and rather than silence, birds and insects filled the air with the cacophony of life.

I'd entered the gates just moments ago, bearing the same weight of desolation I'd felt at my last visit, doubly so because of the burden of the scared, sick world I carried with me. But not long after I shut the car door to set foot on a soft pathway of grass, I was surprised at how welcomed and safe I was feeling, unmasked outside my home for the first time in months with not a single living soul around to fear. With neither thought nor effort, the steel with which I'd reinforced my heart suddenly gave way, and my spirit burst through.

I'd had spiritual insights before, enough to carry me through many a dark night. But this one was different, for in a flash, the entire trajectory of the arc of my life, and the exact locale upon which I was situated, became transparent. Literary studies refers to this as "the big reveal," a resolution of plot that comes late in the narrative and makes explicit that which had previously been withheld from the reader. The big reveal brings to consciousness the secrets that make sense of the entire narrative. What was made known to me that day in the cemetery was no less than the portal to an alternate universe—a secret world inhabited by old souls: a place at once humble and resplendent. I had burst through. And I wasn't alone.

Many of my generation resonate with a growing sense that life had gotten stuck in the dramatic part of the narrative, somewhere short of the resolution for which we had been yearning much of our lives. There is a reason that, back in 1994, sociologist Wade Clark Roof titled his definitive classic about baby boomers *A Generation of Seekers*. His research described the cohort now growing into elderhood as having been motivated by the persistent belief that there had to be more to life than the status quo of the '50s into which our generation had been born. As described in the *New York Times Book Review*, the defining characteristic of the boomer generation has been the lifelong "search for meaning and value in a complex world." In our most recent communication, Professor Roof affirmed that not only has the search continued, but it has been deepened by the passage of close to another 30 years. As our generation of seekers has transited through adulthood and middle and older age, life-experiences for boomers have, as he put it, "led to a more mature spiritual and experiential belief in God . . . ."

Of course, not all has been unrequited yearning. Many of us have built rich lives for ourselves, raising not just one but two generations. There have been joyful times, satisfying relationships, and experiences of life that exceeded expectation. There has been the overcoming of challenges, the learning of humility, and even moments of ecstasy. Our journey thus far has often been exciting and profound. But for Dr. Roof's generation of seekers, this is not enough. We want to know that it has all amounted to something. With all that we expected of ourselves and life, all that we set out to achieve, our diffuse angst continues unabated: the belief that we should be able to do better. Fueled by both yearning and discontent, we reaffirm daily that we will continue to seek for as long as it takes.

Aging, especially in our tumultuous times, has raised the stakes precipitously. Whether the subject at hand centers on environmental disasters and social injustice, disappointments with spouses or adult children, concerns with physical challenges and changing appearances, or thwarted dreams of all stripes and colors, we cannot grasp why after a lifetime of seeking, the harvest we'd expected to reap at our late stage of life has stubbornly eluded us. The world is a mess. We misunderstood so much. And discovering during the pandemic that the mere fact of our age put a target on our backs, we are experiencing the rudest of awakenings. Yet, having invested decades in the journey to culmination, many will testify that there has been some kind of progression through the arc of life. But where is the arrival?

The new understanding of the whole of life I received that day answered this question and many more, showing me a new vision of aging—one where the shadow side of growing older was not a problem to be solved, but the very means of bursting us out of unconsciously held ruts for an experience of longed-for spiritual freedom. This new experience of growing older leaves both denial and aversion in the dust and opens up new space to celebrate age as culmination. Putting what I learned that day into practice, I have come to appreciate this new understanding not just for its intellectual merit but for providing a dependable means by which we can learn to do everything within our power to make serious headway in the fulfillment of life's promise.

It was no accident that the impulse that led to this book took place not only in a cemetery but at the convergence of old age and pandemic. On that day, a good friend in New York had just texted to tell me she had contracted Covid. She turned out to be only the first of many friends, extended family and associates to get the dreaded disease, and not all were to survive. The number of cases in Tennessee had spiked dramatically, competing to be the worst in the country. In retrospect, I see now that the accumulation of circumstances—not just of the day, but of a lifetime—had finally reached critical mass, forcing me over the brink to abject defeat. Clearly, despite years of trying to call the shots, this was not to be my show. I could never be good enough, smart enough, or spiritual enough to count on getting things to turn out for me of my own volition. And incongruously, that was the exact moment a portal to an alternate understanding of the arc of life opened up before me, exposing the truth about my position upon it along with the way forward. Bursting through, I knew instantly that something real happened to me that day, something that, long after, has yet to abate: the much-anticipated but sudden sense that my prayers showing the way to an arrival had been answered. This was most welcomed, but posed the question: *Did it really have to take so long?*

The answer, in a word, is *yes*. There are valid reasons—psychological, biological, societal, and archetypal—for the big reveal to be so long in coming. As many of us who have been working at personal growth for decades discover, it takes nearly a lifetime to get beyond the potent mix of accommodations, denials, illusions, and distractions that constitute what popular culture thinks of as success. But as it turns out, no matter how much love, respect, and achievement you have garnered in the past, the accumulation of years brings insight not only because of that body of experience but, more decisively, because of the disruption aging brings in its wake. As the counterpoint to mastery, there are losses, physical diminishment, and disappointments to be suffered regardless of how invested you have been in working to get things to turn out well for you, those you care for, and the world. Even more unsettling, the very coping strategies that worked for you earlier in life are sooner or later likely to turn against you. By now you have figured out that, the harder you double down, the more elusive the results you thought they'd deliver become.

But there's good news, too. For aging, with all its challenges, also provides the best opportunity life has to offer to recognize that there is something more reliable than the illusion of power to which you have been so tenaciously clinging. You'll know you're approaching bottom, the turning point upon which your experience of life depends, exactly when you are most deeply afraid that you will never bring about what you believe you came here for. But read on. You will discover that even nameless dread can dissipate with the morning dew and that the negative stereotypes of aging, no matter the degree of overlap with your actual circumstances, suddenly become beside the point. Best of all, you will come to recognize that this wondrous place can finally fulfill the promise of a culmination: a place where you are authentic, free, and beloved unconditionally regardless of your past mistakes, current challenges, and concerns about the future. Viewed from this vantage point, you are able to see that, while you may never get what you thought life owed you, you can receive so much more than you'd been settling for.

Many of the academic, spiritual, and mystical traditions to which I've devoted my life allude to this as a sense of a "something more," an apprehension that philosopher Rudolf Otto alluded to in his 1917 work, *The Idea of the Holy*. On the cusp of turning 50, Otto contended that, even when you deconstruct the entire body of spiritual and religious phenomena into scientific understanding, there remains "an overplus of meaning" that refuses to be explained away by rational means. In addition to Otto, there are others who found a way to bridge science and mysticism while somehow managing not to be thrown out of the academy, including Albert Einstein who argued for the existence of a "unified field theory," and William James who, while ambivalent about the existence of God, was unable to deny the possibility of what, akin to Otto, he referred to simply as "more." However one refers to it, seekers intuit that there is a place that promises a deeper, more authentic experience of life—an intimation of the sacred—many years before taking up even temporary residence. We sense its summons even if we can't put this yearning into words. It is this calling that inspires us to explore many paths, everything from meditation and therapy to yoga and any of the plurality of psycho-spiritual offerings from around the world that hold the possibility of delivering answers.

I was such a seeker, wanting to do whatever it would take to experience a spiritual awakening. When I was a teenager, I traveled to Switzerland to sit at the feet of Krishnamurti. In the decades following, I immersed myself in the consciousness-raising movement of the '70s and '80s, both devouring and contributing to the growing body of self-help and inspirational literature. Continuing my psycho-spiritual journey into and through midlife, I got my Master of Theological Studies degree from Vanderbilt Divinity School, followed by my doctorate in the History and Critical Theory of Religion from Vanderbilt University, specializing in the fields of adult and spiritual development. Through it all, I continued writing both academic and personal books about spirituality, seeking to discover what it would take to live life in its intended intensity through all the stages of life. After publishing 30 well-received books, celebrating 50 years married to the same man, raising our two children to independent adulthood, and welcoming two grandsons into the world, I had to admit I'd experienced my share of success and happiness. But no matter how hard I tried, something felt fundamentally off: the missing piece that would make sense of it all.

I wouldn't have expected the isolation of Covid to provide the answers that had evaded me. But as I acclimated myself to life in sequester and began reaching out beyond my inner circle, I discovered something unexpected. Many of my peers reported experiencing a similar spiritual quickening right around the same time, hand in hand with a deepening sense of the immediacy of crisis, as an out-of-control virus put to the test our beliefs about legacy, meaning, and purpose. It wasn't until I took that life-changing walk that I came to understand that many of us were experiencing the same pathos of failed expectations simultaneously and perhaps had been for quite awhile without my knowing it. But now, through the alchemy of this double dose of age and pandemic, we were waking up to our authentic selves. It was as though our innate potential for spiritual growth was catalyzing us into a secret society of old souls, having transited through the challenges of all the life stages to this moment. Now, in the most unexpected of times, places, and ways, we were finally beginning to make sense of the entire arc of life, finding ourselves together on territory that was at once uncharted and strangely familiar.

When the invitation to cross over into this secret world of aging was issued to me, I experienced the sense of bursting through as a gift of grace. Of course, in the coming months, the intensity of the inflow of merger with the Divine was to come and go, like waves lapping gently on a shore. But even as the waves of understanding swept back out to sea, carrying notions of perfection with them, enough seashells remained behind to remind me that what I'd experienced was real. And that, even if I have not been changed perfectly, there was at least the hint of something new birthing that could not be denied. And not just for me—for many of us.

Looking at the life cycle through the dual lenses of scholarship and mysticism, I'm quick to concede that this enriched understanding of older age runs counter to the norm. Some will think the encounter with this alternate universe of aging to be improbable, irrational, or even desperate. But this is only true to the degree that fear of aging has been fueled by inadequate models of the life cycle held by social scientists, gerontologists, marketers, and popular culture. The mainstream canon of adult and spiritual development theory that has come to us through academia is adept at describing how people grow through childhood or adolescence, but it only occasionally touches upon the transition into middle age and, even more rarely, beyond. And based in the social sciences, the theorists are far more ready to credit biology and social influences as spurs through life stages than spiritual forces, let alone the Divine. For most, old age, defined as anything beyond midlife, is implicitly a developmental wasteland devoid of meaning, purpose, or value. It is no accident that negative stereotypes of aging dominate, whether they manifest as marginalization, exploitation, denial, denigration, or romanticizing. But the existing life-stage models don't lead us to a misunderstanding only of the final life stage, but of the spiritual trajectory of the entire lifespan. Hampered by incomplete models that stop short of old age, our normal understanding of adult development has turned just about everything that matters most pretty much upside down. *The Making of an Old Soul* is an opportunity to turn things right side up again.

The day I drove through the cemetery gates, I had never felt so alone. Yet this was the wretched condition in which, moments later, a beam of inspiration broke open my heart, engraving the missing piece that made sense of it all, writ large. What I glimpsed that day is that the most important part of spiritual development could never be contained in the span of any single life. Rather, it is mystical consciousness that both infuses and transcends life itself: something eternal and sustaining, often defying the apparent circumstances we're facing at any given time, that leads us to intuit that this *something more* is a force for good in our lives. This is the alpha and the omega of merger with the Divine: the undifferentiated consciousness that predates our inception, to which we return upon dying and which urges us forward toward awakening throughout the course of our lives.

This is what I experienced that day at the cemetery and that had been presaged by every mystical encounter I've had over the course of my life, as if invisible hands had been passing me forward along the way to some unknown but yearned-for destination. In the pages following you will find this revisioned understanding of the arc of life: 11 stages of adult and spiritual development. These developmental stages include but transcend the classic progression described by the social sciences, illuminating and completing the life cycle as viewed from a heightened state of mystical consciousness. In this fresh revelation, old age is the culmination: a life stage that is not a coda, not an afterthought, but the very point of life.

This alternate view of aging constitutes the secret world of old souls where you can come to embrace the luminous spirit within that beats steadily beyond the wounds of childhood, beyond the unintended consequences of even your best intentions, beyond the twists and turns of fate, over which even at the peak of the developmental pyramid you have no control. In the end, *The Making of an Old Soul* shows the way to become receptive to getting what you came here for: and *something more*.

— PART TWO —

The Arc of Life

The Eleven Stages of Adult and Spiritual Development

"Only you can take your journey . . . . But you must know there are many others on the same voyage, with similar wreckage behind as well, facing similar fears, and riddled with similar self-doubt. And still, the open sea, the realm of the imaginally limitless beckons. All we can do is show up, grab an oar, do the best we can, and, while alone, sail this same sibilant sea together."

—James Hollis, *Living Between Worlds*

WE NOW KNOW THAT YOUR YEARNING for something more is all for the good and can be trusted. And so it is that I wish you a safe and easy journey through life. But history, both personal and communal, reports that not all the storms are behind us and that, more often than not, the sea upon which we've set forth will toss us about, waves lashing first our bow, then our stern. An oar is useful, of course, but won't help all that much if we don't have some idea of where we're headed.

When I embarked upon my doctoral studies in the fields of adult and spiritual development, I was drawn forward by the promise of encountering a predictable progression through life. I learned a lot, and yet the answers I sought continued to elude me: *How can I harness this information to quicken my pace and ensure my own arrival to the highest stages of psycho-social development?* And equally important: *How will I know when I've arrived?* The social scientists got us this far in life, and now it is time for the mystics, the sages, spiritual and recovery practices, and the Conscious Aging movement to join in. We also need the stories of old souls—those hearty adventurers who have walked close to the edge and lived to tell the tale. Memoirists and essayists like Florida Scott-Maxwell, Parker J. Palmer, Joan Chittister, John C. Robinson, Harry R. Moody, Robert L. Weber, Connie Goldman, Ram Dass, Zalman Schachter-Shalomi, and so many more, whether still living or of blessed memory, give us not only their stories but hope to light the way. Taken together, neither do the scientists and mystics abrogate one another but, rather, they connect, complement, and complete a new understanding of the progression through life stages leading to old age as culmination.

What I learned that day in the cemetery is that this transformation into an old soul will not be something you will have to work to master. It will not require personal power. Rather, the vision of the arc of life I'm about to share with you will be more akin to a tuning fork: something with which you will resonate. You won't need to make this happen—you can only give into it. This is the final piece of adult development theory that has been missing, and that answers what I now believe to be the most important question of all: *Am I willing to accept the invitation to grow that has already been issued?* Don't answer too quickly, for responding in the affirmative will require you to question every illusion in which you ever took refuge; to rethink the most fondly protected fundamentals of your beliefs; to let go of your habitual attempts to maintain control. Though this book is titled *The Making of an Old Soul,* answering the invitation will not be just a recipe or a prescription, but a leap of faith. While this is a leap each one of us must make alone, happily there are the way-showers who have gone over the edge before us and returned with words of assurance that there is more to life than we have been settling for, and that, when we find it, it will be good.

However efficient or involved your journey may be, honor yourself for having gotten this far. Grab onto your oar as lovingly as possible and trust in the unfolding promise the future holds for all who dare to rise to the occasion that life brings to us every day of our lives.

— STAGE I —

Merged with the Divine

WE ARE READY TO BEGIN our revisioned journey through life stages, the alchemical transformation of science and mystical consciousness into something at once very old and brand-new. We take our most radical departure from the social sciences right from the get-go: this first stage of development. While traditional life stage models logically begin with birth, the big reveal I received that day on my walk through the cemetery intuited something a priori, not just important, but critical to understanding how human beings grow through time psychologically and spiritually. To wit, to be truly complete and accurate, the new model needs to take us beyond the boundaries of empirical knowledge to consider: where do we come from before we are conceived, and where do we go after we die? While at this point of human history we will have to seek our answers in the realm of the *something more* we spoke of earlier, we do find ourselves, comfortingly, standing not only in the shadow of the mystics but on the cutting edge of science.

Before we bring in the scientists, your own experience as a lifelong seeker has given you first-hand knowledge of the diffuse yearning that has propelled your search for what is missing in your life. In response, the mystics challenge you with a simple question: *How can you miss what you have never known?* Seen through the mystic's eyes, yearning is, in truth, a tug backwards: a particular and poignant homesickness. In metaphysical circles, the answer takes form as the argument for the existence of an undifferentiated consciousness from whence we come. The conviction of something beyond ordinary consciousness is most apparent in the near-universal fascination with the possibility of an afterlife. Less voice is given to questions about what comes before we are born. Some theologians believe that we all have a soul that will not only last into eternity, but that has always existed; others believe that the soul comes into existence at some point just before or during conception, in the womb, or upon one's first breath. (It is perhaps no accident that the Hebrew word "ruach" is not only the word for breath, but also the word for life and spirit.)In Christianity, the notion of pre-existence is highly controversial. Based on Biblical passages, Origen, a second- and third-century church father, argued for it, citing, amongst others, Jeremiah 1:5: "Before I formed thee in the belly I knew thee; and before thou camest forth out of the womb I sanctified thee . . . ." The Second Council of Constantinople disagreed, and the doctrine of pre-existence was condemned as heresy.

Pre-existence fares better in Hinduism. For instance, in the Bhagavad Gita, Krishna tells Arjuna: "Never was there a time when I did not exist, nor you, nor all these kings; nor in the future shall any of us cease to be." This stream of thought surfaces again in the work of author and spiritual teacher Ram Dass and in contemporary New Age spirituality, with its references to one's "choosing to be born." "You took birth here because you had certain work to do. This is your curriculum.

It's not an error. Where you are now with all your neuroses and your problems, you're sitting in just the right place," writes Ram Dass. In New Age philosophy, whether addressed implicitly or merely implied, there is the widely held belief that, at some point, the soul had been merged with the Divine in a state of undifferentiated consciousness, out of which the choice to separate into an individual ego with a differentiated consciousness was undertaken. Yet again, we are marched to the edge of a new set of challenging questions. For what exactly, then, are we differentiating from? In others words, *What is consciousness?*

On the most basic level, we have the *Oxford English Dictionary* definition of consciousness as "the state of being awake and aware of one's surroundings." But over the course of several centuries, the meaning of the word has both evolved and complexified. And here, at last, we encounter the brave cadre of credentialed scientists who are studying the nature of consciousness: *What is it, how does it function and when does consciousness begin?* Researchers are drawn from the cognitive sciences, involving fields such as psychology, linguistics, anthropology, neuropsychology, and neuroscience. In medical circles, definitions of consciousness take an immediate practical turn, as physicians aim to rate an incapacitated patient's ability to respond to stimuli on a continuum from "capable of complete comprehension" through "comatose."

An epicenter of consciousness studies is IONS, the Institute of Noetic Sciences, founded by Apollo 14 astronaut, astrophysicist, and engineer Dr. Edgar Mitchell with the specific goal of submitting the study of consciousness to scientific research and testing. Mitchell, amongst the first astronauts to walk on the moon, had a mystical experience en route back to earth. As shared on the IONS website, "Dr. Edgar Mitchell had the profound experience of feeling interconnected to everything he was observing from the window of his space capsule: the stars, the moon, our blue planet, and the vastness of the cosmos. He realized quickly that in order to explain such an extraordinary experience (and others like it), there would need to be a rapprochement between the scientific and spiritual interpretations of reality." Nevertheless, despite a plethora of scholarly papers, conferences, and coordinated research across a wide range of institutions, the burgeoning field of consciousness studies has yet to countervail the prevailing scientific premise that consciousness is nothing more than an illusion created by the brain.

Whether calling upon faith or science for validation, there is at least one thing many of us can agree upon. When considering the entirety of the timeline of prior to the fertilized egg through early infancy, there is some point at which a qualitative change in consciousness transpires as the individual becomes self-aware. For purposes of this discussion, when this takes place is less relevant than the fact that separation from undifferentiated consciousness into an individuated ego takes place at all.

We turn our attention now to the second stage of development, arguably both the most painful and the most important thing that will ever happen to us over the course of our lives in service of the making of an old soul.

— STAGE 2 —

Separation: The Original Wound

WHEN I WAS SEVEN, the junior rabbi shared a story with the children of our congregation that has stayed with me for over 65 years. "Why does a baby cry when he's born?" he asked. "Because before he's born, he knows everything about everything, but when the doctor slaps his bottom to take his first breath, he knocks it all out of him."

This equation of birth with loss would be enough to make anybody cry. But this sense of separation that we experience from the beginning is not just a matter of philosophical debate or theological musing, but one of sheer physical pain. Being born hurts, and there are many good reasons why, in healthy development, one's first act upon expulsion from the womb is to howl.

Doctors don't actually slap the newborn routinely anymore to facilitate the child's first breath, but what difference does that really make when that intake of air feels like your lungs have been set on fire? But by then, you will have already endured the painful process of being born. Pushed, pummeled, punched and ultimately shoved into the cold, you will then be forced to squint against the glaring light with un-used eyes. If you are one of the lucky ones, it may be mere moments before you're laid upon the soft, welcoming skin of that which you had previously known from inside out—mother. But nevertheless—and no matter how gently it may be administered—there will all too soon be an onslaught of tubes, swabs, cold metal instruments, and all manner of invasion. Plus, adding insult to injury, you're not only born hungry, crying to be fed, but from now on, you will have to work for it.

It is no coincidence that some theologians believe the story of expulsion of Adam and Eve from the Garden of Eden to be a metaphor for leaving the womb. But, in this story, this separation from merger with the Divine was not ascribed to be the consequence of biology or even bad luck, but of punishment. Taking a page from my junior rabbi's story, Eve, in eating of the forbidden fruit, aims to regain all the knowledge in one bite that had figuratively been slapped out of her. Christian theology takes it one step further, asserting that in acting on that urge, human beings had committed the original sin. While the nuances and interpretations of original sin vary widely over the centuries and from one denomination to another, the norm of Christian doctrine purports that, because of what happened in that garden, humans have inherited a tainted nature. Symbolic stories of expulsion from the Divine into separation as punishment find their way into the scriptures and texts of multiple religious and spiritual formulations, so universal as to be considered archetypal. In psychological terms, the pain of separation is referred to as a primal wound experienced at one end of the spectrum as a threat to one's very survival. At the other end, the wound manifests as a concept with which by now you will undoubtedly be familiar: the persistent yearning for something intangible gone missing. But, regardless of how the wound plays out in any particular individual's life, there is a conclusion all humans arrive at, so pernicious and onerous that for most of our lives it cannot be embraced gracefully. In a nutshell, the core misunderstanding is this: *Something's gone wrong and I am responsible.*

We will discover when we move onto the stages that follow hard upon *Separation*, that how you choose to respond to this both unbearable and mistaken conclusion will be influenced by many factors that are beyond your control. These include but are not limited to the quality of parenting you received; the environment, belief systems, and circumstances into which you were born; your health and genetic predisposition; and so on. But, arguably, even more critical will be how you respond to the unwanted things that happen to you. These responses, decisions and choices—some made consciously but many instinctually—will set in motion a series of events, implications, side-effects, and ramifications that will determine not only the direction of your life but the pace and quality of your journey toward psychological and spiritual growth. This is the modus operandi: the inexorable impact equivalent of the Big Bang that will continue to unfold throughout as many stages in the arc of life that are necessary until you become able and willing to see your erroneous conclusion for what it is, and to take corrective action.

The nature of the original misunderstanding is often hidden in plain sight, in the form of the story of your birth as shared by your mother and other narrators of the drama of your life. Some children are born premature, ripped from their mother's arms and placed in an incubator, left to try to figure it all out without even the temporary reprieve of a reassuring touch. Others, on the other hand, are told that they practically slid straight from womb to breast, eyes wide open in wonder. But even the mythical happiest newborns—the "rainbow" children who appear regularly in New Age accounts—cry when they're hungry, cold, wet, or gassy. If they don't, that too becomes a matter of concern.

In my own birth story, the misunderstanding of the role I played, and the harm it caused, is explicit. My mother, like many of her generation, powered her way through the Great Depression and World War II and into the safe harbor of the postwar suburbs. She did so by dint of her most prized attribute—an iron will—before giving birth to me. The Jewish wife of a doctor, how she ended up in a Catholic hospital that withheld pain medicine for philosophical reasons remains a mystery. But needless to say, my birth story centers largely on how long the labor and how large the pain. Over the course of many years of introspection, I have come to understand that, through no fault of my own, my mother took the pain of my birth as a personal affront: a hard pill to swallow, not only for a woman who prided herself on her ability to overcome whatever challenges came her way, but for me, her daughter, who grew up wanting only to please her mother and not knowing why every effort was doomed from the start. In my birth narrative, the adoption of unwarranted responsibility is explicit. For others, the story of one's fall from grace is more subtle—or denied. It took not years or even decades but most of my life to consciously surface just how hard I'd been on myself from the beginning.

For me, for many of us, what the rabbi's doctor metaphorically slapped out of us at birth was the knowledge of our own fundamental goodness. Your journey through the arc of life begins with your expulsion from merger with the Divine through birth, accompanied by an initiatory trial of pain and suffering. As I wrote earlier, until this resurfaces again for you to deal with consciously toward journey's end, this may be the most important thing that ever happened to you. But it is not the most interesting. For that, the true initiation of the uniquely creative story of your life, a tale of heights and depths, missteps and corrections, chastisement and heroism, you'll need to turn the page to Stage 3: *The Personality Project.*

The Personality Project

Y OU ARRIVE AT THE THIRD DEVELOPMENTAL STAGE wet, hungry, and separated from the only home you have ever known. The question now becomes, *What are you going to do about it?* On the most practical level, instinct kick-starts the quest for mastery over your circumstances. Think of your first howl as not only a response to discomfort but an experiment, the success upon which your very survival depends. Will your basic demands be met? As instinct merges with incipient but conscious will, even the newborn has the capacity to gather information and assess results. This is the initiation of a process of trial and error that will be guided henceforth by the apparent connection between your actions and their outcomes.

Your degree of success will be, of course, not solely the result of the robustness of your demands, but also determined by the trustworthiness of a caring source attentive to and capable of fulfilling your needs. But being born to parents whose idea of what you need matches your own is hardly a given. Many of us born in the postwar era were subjected to the parenting norms of the day that privileged discipline, deferment of gratification, and the development of moral fiber over the infant's natural desire to be held and fed on demand. The baby was left to whimper for food if the clock said it wasn't time yet and shut away in her room to cry herself to sleep at nap and bedtime. Even hugging was meant to be kept to a minimum lest the offspring become "spoiled."

Not every mom in the suburban '50s followed this childrearing norm, and certainly when we, their offspring, had children of our own, we mostly did everything as polar opposite as possible. We hugged, we praised, and we indulged, undoubtedly to a fault. Differences in parenting styles, philosophies and dispositions—whatever the generational norm—inspire varying responses as even the youngest child quickly learns to repeat those behaviors that get better results. For instance, when cooing proves to be more effective than a howl at producing a breast, the baby may quickly come to understand that her ticket to happiness is to coo more, howl less. If this describes you, as you began to make a habit of sweet sounds, smiles, and general affability, you became the "easy child". Easy you may have appeared to be, but deep down you would be hard at work correcting qualities and behaviors deemed by others to be unattractive or unproductive. This is the middle schooler who is popular with his friends, voted "best in class" in high school, "a natural born leader" in college, and eventually "employee of the year" at work. His success will have been won at a cost, as he learns from his earliest days to override his inconveniencing needs: keeping quiet when his instinct is to cry, shout, or sing ebulliently, so as not to disturb.

On the other hand, the child whose sweet intonations go unheeded will need to raise the decibel level in order to get the attention he requires. Needless to say, the latter may have to work that much harder at getting his needs met. Whereas the easy child grows up to be best in class, the difficult child is deemed a trouble-maker. Some of us who were tagged too noisy, too demanding, or too curious might have wished to walk a sunnier path through life but fell short for any number of reasons. Many of us, unable to manage the building and maintenance of one of the prettier masks, got our needs met from one of the less desirable ones plucked from the remainder bin. While you may have been tagged early on as a problem child, you may have, in truth, simply been more acutely aware than others of your authentic needs and wants, less willing to make compromises. Who you really are sneaked out through the cracks of haphazardly constructed masks whether you wished it would or not.

Here, we come to the crux of the third stage of development: that, if you are fortunate enough to have been tapped by fate to become a seeker, you will spend much of your life trying to regain what was lost by outsmarting, manipulating, and exercising whatever personal power you can muster to set things right. As trial and error accelerates, the original wound goes largely underground. But it does not disappear. In fact, having gotten the ball rolling, primal fears and yearnings continue to call the shots, mostly unconsciously, in a grand experiment: the building of a personality. This is the foundational drive that pushes you through the primary tasks of childhood and adolescence into adulthood, your efforts becoming increasingly sophisticated as you invest in the core project of your life: inventing a Self.

The personality-building project starts simply and organically enough. And over time, instinctual responses become habit if they appear to succeed at quelling the sharper edges of your anxieties, and help you get at least your basic needs met. You do not consciously experience yourself as an individual who has adopted these behaviors and attitudes that diverge from your authentic self in order to survive. Rather, you come to identify with your habits completely. As the years unfold, personality strategies thicken and congeal into concrete masks that provide sufficient cover to survive, but that let neither air or light into the hidden depths where the authentic self is left to fend for itself. This, then, is Stage 3: the developmental ground zero where not only do you have masks but, more to the point, where the masks have you.

The task of building a personality will dominate and determine the trajectory of your life until you evolve sufficiently to have some say over the matter. Until then, your response to your original wound, and the chain of dominoes it set in motion, will in great part determine how other people see you and how you see yourself. The performative aspect may earn you acceptance or not, but in this developmental stage, the power to affirm or deny resides outside of you, in the form of others' opinion, be it parents, teachers, peer group, or society as a whole. Though hard-won, that which is so dependent on external forces can also be taken away. Whether assuming form in the shadows of the child's nightmares or bubbling to the surface in the teenager's locked diary, there is the diffuse sense that there is a discrepancy between who you are, what you want, and what you have to do to get your needs met. You continue to be pushed from behind by unconscious forces, working hard to keep one step ahead of your anxiety.

Of course, sometimes you succeed. You figure some things out, and they work well and long enough for you to feel powerful, at least for a while. And, too, every once in a while you get lucky. Things turn out just as you'd hoped. And here the grand experiment can take a metaphysical turn. When good things happen that don't seem to connect with your personal efforts, you will take a stab at replicating the circumstances and behaviors that appear to correlate, even if you are being irrational. If you were wearing red, not blue, to the sock hop when your first crush asked you to dance, red rather than blue might well become your favorite color. Thus, the quirks of fate, and your attempts to replicate luck by dint of your own will, also become part of the personality-building process. In the same way, you may make a special effort to avoid stepping on cracks, hold your breath when passing a cemetery, and the like: magical thinking is destined to be squeezed into your overstuffed bag of coping strategies in the effort to maximize the potential for good.

In this way, the personality under formation incorporates a variety of incipient superstitious and religious impulses. Some are overt, such as the child praying beside her bed to make it through the night. But others shape us without our conscious participation. In these early years, you are laying the foundation for beliefs and attitudes that will continue to impact you for many developmental stages to come, and often without your knowledge or assent. Again, in this, you will be influenced greatly by the religious beliefs and practices within which you are raised. But few, regardless of upbringing, will avoid conceptualizing a relationship with a power greater than yourself that is in one way or another at least partly dysfunctional. For instance, you may be sold in Sunday school on the notion of God's unconditional love, but you will probably be a lot more worried about whether your behavior has bought you a one-way ticket straight to hell. Replicating the history of religion in our own inherited complex of possible responses, you adopt habits early on designed to appease, you make deals in the form of sacrifice, asceticism, or overcompensation; and, even when you attempt to be good, to help or even save others, it will often be to win approval or for other ego-bolstering reasons. These too become incorporated into your identity.

I vividly recall at the age of five standing on the concrete basement floor of my childhood home, listening through the bottom end of the aluminum laundry chute to my mother and my older brother arguing upstairs. Dream analysts will appreciate the richness of the imagery in my retelling, basements often symbolizing our unconscious thoughts—but this memory was all too real. It was a recurring event in our house: the more my mother berated my stoic brother to become the extrovert she preferred, the stonier he got. I could not understand why he would just not give her what she was asking for: it would just be so easy to babble on about how his exam went, play the piano for company, and cause peace everlasting to rain down upon our house. But on that particular day, the metal chute amplifying the tension, I made a solemn vow. However reserved my brother was, I would compensate. If he was quiet, I'd be noisy. If he was withholding, I'd be abundant. If he refused to entertain, I'd be the star of the show. I was sure that in this way my mother would finally get her needs met, the family would be fixed once and for all, and I'd get the credit. There was one hitch to the plan. In a culture and family that privileges first-born brothers above all, be it Jacob over Esau or Prince William over Harry, I was invisible. Being a girl, doubly so. But that didn't stop me from trying. Did I succeed? Partially. I did become emotionally abundant and a stellar performer. However, even on her deathbed, as I sat alone at her side day after day like Horton the Elephant, "faithful one hundred per cent," Mom got the final word. "I know why your brother isn't here," she said to me, just before passing. "You suck all the air out of the room."

All my life, from age five on, I'd had only the best intentions, but even our best efforts can mark us for life, falling short of fixing whatever we perceive as broken. If this were all it is, one would look upon this stage of the arc of life in a dim light indeed. But, as we've learned from the mystics, there is also "something more." What is it, in the trial-and-error process, that gets us up in the morning to try again? What accounts for the creativity and resilience we bring to our challenges? How is it that we believe that sooner or later we will get it right, even if our idea of "right" bears little in common with what we will eventually discover is what we have truly been yearning for?

Throughout my theological education, I was fascinated by a question that led me to my specialization in the fields of adult and spiritual development: *Why are some willing to accept the invitation to grow spiritually while others refuse?* During my time in grad school, I found hundreds of theories, explanations, and beliefs that aimed to answer this question. But preserved in my notebooks, circled in red and punctuated with an exclamation mark, was a passage that provided the most satisfying answer. It was a summary of the theological work of philosopher and mathematician Alfred North Whitehead. You will recall from my earlier discussion of Stages 1 and 2 of the arc of life, that as part of my revelation I saw birth not just as the beginning of life but as a turning point, initiating separation from merger with the Divine and the beginning of the unfolding of one's unique life story. In accordance with Whitehead's Process Theology, I witnessed that your progression through life stages, everything that will subsequently happen in your life—internal and external—is set in motion by this Big Bang event. Every moment arises out of all that has preceded it. While the past culminates in each present moment, the past does not wholly determine the future because in the present moment, the individual is free to make choices that introduce novel elements into the mix. Present, too, in every moment is the tendency for good to prevail. This, for me, is God—the *something more* that tips the balance, inviting us to make the best possible choice: the most loving, life-giving decision, regardless of our past conditioning and circumstances. Stated simply, we have a reservoir of intuition and wisdom ready to be tapped to provide us with the opportunity to actualize the best possibility available to us in every situation—"best" meaning the choice most in keeping with divine love.

Because you are free, however, you do not automatically respond to the impulse for good. You can reject, ignore, or block the reception of it in favor of any of the myriad possibilities that freedom—free will—makes available to you. Divine love urges you toward the greatest good possible, and it is this that inspires you forward through the developmental progression. It urges you, but it doesn't force you. If your freedom is real, then so is your potential to make poor choices resulting in added suffering and pain.

"Increasing the freedom of the creatures was risky on God's part," John B. Cobb Jr. and David Ray Griffin write in *Process Theology*, their helpful book about Whitehead. "But it was a necessary risk, if there was to be the chance for greatness." What is the deciding factor that turns one toward rather than away from the greatest good? It is your intention to do what is right and best, and that this can be enough to shift the odds in your favor for the greatest possible success. In traditional religious language, this deciding factor is your trust in God. But even those who are averse to religious language can resonate with the notion that your mere willingness to entertain hope can itself make the difference. There is nothing you can do to guarantee particular outcomes, but you can come to believe that something beyond your current level of insight and discernment cannot only show you the best possible choice for yourself but persuade you to make it. This mysterious expanded awareness does not take note of temporal appearances of mastery and success, but seems only to care for the long game: the grinding of the rock of ego to the luminosity of soul. This *something more*—that which is encountered in the midst of the leap of faith and, in truth, that which nudged you over the edge into the unknown in the first place—is the essential element that can always be trusted to act upon the past to create anew.

While I encountered Process Theology in the course of my academic studies, it was beyond the walls of institutional learning that I discovered a realm of elders and mystics who had made this theology not just an intellectual construct but a way of life, one that is open to those of us who are not only growing old but becoming more conscious. It may be many years before you come to understand what the best choice at any particular time might have been. But even your unrequited desires and false starts can pile up like water behind the dam, invisible from the other side. Yet, as it rises to the top, all it needs to get things flowing in the right direction again is one single drop of faith. Be it hope or a cry for help, there is something about those of us who are on the road to becoming old souls that is indomitable: our twin hearts of discontent and persistence, animated by an impulse that is no more nor no less than the yearning for fulfillment.

We can all come to appreciate the efficiency and resourcefulness each of us has brought to bear against the varying degrees of intolerable situations we have faced, necessitating moment-by-moment creativity in order to survive. Even if we experience our lives as full of U-turns and dead-ends, *The Making of an Old Soul* assures us that it was all for the good. In the hope that has sustained us through it all, we will eventually come to recognize a Power greater than ourselves at work in our lives. Not the power driven by fear, adopted in the vulnerability of childhood, but the unconditional source of love we will come to know in the more advanced stages of psychological and spiritual growth that is inexorably drawing us forward.

But first we have a number of additional developmental stages through which we must transit, beginning with the next life stage, *Unintended Consequences*.

— STAGE 4 —

Unintended Consequences

YOU ADOPTED YOUR PARTICULAR MASKS for a reason, and as long as your masks serve a purpose, you continue to hide your authentic self behind them. If your masks are performing adequately, short of intervention—divine or otherwise—you will lack sufficient impetus to advance. Ironically, the more successful your mask, the longer you may stay stuck in the fourth developmental stage, perhaps for the entirety of your life.

Such was the case of a fellow author who became a confidante late in life, just months before her passing. Secretly nicknaming her Queen Bee, I was envious of her big bestseller, so early in her career, on subject matter that overlapped with my own. While she'd always been polite when we crossed paths at book conventions and conferences, she both demanded and received a level of deference that somehow eluded me. Then, out of the blue, she called to ask me something, requesting that I keep it confidential.

She wanted to know if I could introduce her to my agent. Here she'd given the impression that she was all set with one of the biggest agents in the world. But who knew that this was just a fancy mask, hiding a secret? Despite her work's classic status, the sales had dwindled precipitously. Her agent, who had finally given up asking her for a new book, had quietly cut her loose years ago. What Bee told me over the course of our hour-long call was that she had stopped writing not because she was content to ride side-saddle on the back of her bestseller through life, but because she was too proud and too scared to write a book proposal that could be rejected. Rather than come down off her pedestal to commiserate and network with her less luminous fellow authors, she stalled out.

Never once during our many years crisscrossing paths had she let her impeccable hair down long enough to learn that virtually all her fellow authors carried either that concern or variations on the theme. We just hadn't struck gold big enough to carry off the most dazzling mask of all: becoming "a name." While we were busy envying her success, she had been secretly admiring our camaraderie, persistence, and courage, as we churned out book after book only to be stuck with a pitcher on the panelist table while she sipped Perrier at the podium. The best-selling mask she had so carefully constructed and maintained to avoid any chance of rejection brought about exactly what she most feared: marginalization. While I gladly shared my agent's name with her, there was to be no next book.

Like Queen Bee, sooner or later you will have been confronted with something most unexpected. The very masks that provide the most complete cover are at the same time the ones most likely to create unintended consequences that bring about exactly what you'd most been hoping to protect yourself from. I suffered my first memorable unintended consequence in junior high, wanting nothing more than to be popular but not knowing how. I disguised my vulnerability under a mask cobbled together out of accomplishments—honors track, first-

chair clarinet in band and orchestra, an editor of the yearbook—
only to discover years later that at least one of the in-crowd
kids who wanted to be my friend had felt too intimidated
to reach out. If you don't see it, you can't fix it. And so it is
that the fourth stage of development—admitting to suffering
unintended consequences stemming from even your most
successful constructions—represents essential progress.

These unintended consequences include:

- Masks that use force or deception to simulate power
  (the bully, the popular one) may achieve what looks
  like "success" but trigger others' resentment.

- Masks of superiority provide an explanation for
  one's loneliness but trigger others' envy or fear of
  rejection.

- Masks of compliance aim to be perceived as
  generosity, acceptance, and love but may be read as
  weakness and invite abuse.

- Masks built around helping others distance them
  by generating resistance to the presumption of
  unearned authority.

As unintended consequences increasingly test your best
efforts to keep your masks intact, it becomes harder and harder
to maintain an airtight facade. Even if you can fool others, the
truth is dawning on you. Your masks have cracks. Ironically,
entry to increased consciousness is through the very cracks that
have begun to show: the exact gates through which you would
probably least like to pass. There is a special opportunity when,
due to crisis, rifts suddenly appear in layers that solidified into
ego years ago. It is through these burgeoning cracks that you
can get a glimpse of your authentic self and of the harm you
have inadvertently caused yourself and others. This is a painful

process and may, in fact, feel even more painful than the original wound your masks were meant to remedy. Self-awareness, at any age, is hard-won indeed, requiring a level of courage and honesty that is rarely your first choice and often resorted to only when every other strategy has come up short.

Fortunately, you do not need to let all your masks drop away either completely or all at once for the work of psycho-spiritual development to continue apace. As your developmental journey continues, you may be found at times holding onto particular masks, even if they are destructive, because the alternative— losing protective cover—is too painful to contemplate. However long and hard-fought the struggle, gaining access to whatever increase in consciousness you can bring to bear on excavating your authentic self from the crumbling masks is a gift of grace.

Earlier, I referred to those of us driven by discontent as lucky because our pain can be counted upon to point us in the general direction of where we need to go. As the developmental stages unfold, an inexorable logic has to play out over long periods of time. There is no hurrying the process, and nothing is wasted. You learn from every choice, good and bad, and from every circumstance you endure, whether or not you get the resolution you'd thought you wanted most. Regardless of how much more challenging you judge your journey through life to be in comparison to that of others, let us take a moment to celebrate how far you've come, having managed expulsion from the womb, the construction of a personality, and living long enough to have suffered unintended consequences. You have done all this even while bearing a mortal wound. And given that you are reading these words now, I have encouraging news for you. Your primary objective—to get your basic needs met— succeeded, or you wouldn't have survived. But for seekers like us, basic satisfaction will never be enough. For you knew it from the very beginning, and are even more certain of it now: there is something more.

There will be an organic unfolding at the exact right time, place, and pace for you, including a fair share of detours, setbacks, and dead-ends. But there will also be leaps forward, revelations and grace, often when you are least expecting them. However convoluted the journey, when the emotional ramifications can no longer be ignored, you will enter a period of potentially escalating spiritual growth that will propel you forward. Meanwhile, you will continue to question, to struggle, to yearn: and all these are signs that you are well on your way.

— STAGE 5 —

Exercising Power

I F WE COULD SIMPLY SKIP from Stage 4, *Unintended Consequences*, to Stage 6, *Dismantling Your Masks*, and beyond, this book would not need to be about age as culmination. You would have long ago admitted to powerlessness, embraced your authentic self, made appropriate reparations, and fulfilled life's promise. Culmination could theoretically occur at any age. But not so fast. For it is here, in Stage 5, that even all the while knowing better, you can't help but give your masks and their promise of protection one more try. This time, you won't just double down, trying harder to do more of what didn't work all that well in the first place. Rather, you will attempt acts of power at once so dazzling and deceptive that you may well be stuck in them not just for years, but for decades. The final masks you adopt before the whole mess of defenses and accusations you constructed goes down in flames don't just whirl away. They cycle through, again and again, until you are finally old enough, exhausted enough, and desperate enough to stop peddling. You know just enough to confront the uncomfortable truth that you have bent yourself into distorted shapes in an attempt at life mastery that has caused you and others collateral damage. And that you are sick and tired of it.

In healthy development, this exhaustion manifests as the urge to break with the past and try new ways of interacting with the world: to tune in to what you really want and then go for it. You may move away from home, initiate a break-up, or take up a spiritual path. But more often than not, in Stage 5, your bolt to freedom turns out to be not so much novel as reactive. As unskilled as you are energetic, whatever it is you wish to leave behind, your way forward will by and large be determined by doing pretty much the opposite. If you married the man of your mother's dreams, you may find yourself having an affair with the gardener. You may drop out of your role as the good suburban housewife and move to a commune. In Stage 5, you are likely to make bad choices primarily to prove that you are your own person. The transition to this stage in its own way represents a progression, but one that creates as many or even more problems than it solves. If this advancement happens to coincide with the adolescent years, you become a rebel. If later, you may experience this as midlife crisis. And don't be surprised if the urge to exercise your power cycles through not just occasionally but over and over again, taking the form of yet one more attempt at reinvention late in life. But each cycle bears the same archetypal hallmark: dissatisfaction with your previous conditioning and with those to whom you ascribe blame. This comes coupled with the belief that, in breaking from the status quo, you can do better.

You will get a rush of adrenalin from each act of rebellion, and you will interpret this to mean that you have succeeded in healing the rifts of the past to arrive at the portal to freedom. But here's the rub. To the degree your actions have been formed in reaction to what came before, you are not truly free. It is the past that is still determining your actions, but now, instead of acquiescing, you are compelled to respond with a knee-jerk reactivity masquerading as free will. You have succeeded only in the construction of an even thicker mask layered upon a crumbling persona in a haphazard and often faltering effort to tend to the cracks. Your revolt, while genuine, will have served only to initiate a new but increasingly disappointing cycle that creates its own unintended consequences and that avoids rather than addresses the mistaken, unconsciously held belief in your essential wrongness.

The reason one can get stalled in Stage 5 for so long is that it seems, for all the world, as if you have achieved freedom, godliness, or even martyrdom, while you have merely donned one of the more sophisticated masks, one of particular allure to seekers. We are talking here about the spiritual mask, trickiest of them all to see and even trickier to crack. You will know you are still wearing a mask when you think of yourself as enlightened, spiritually advanced, transcendent, or awake—and yet, in the secret recesses of your heart, something is missing.

There will be a time, as you advance through the progressing stages in the arc of life, that will feel like an arrival. And when you do, regardless of the circumstances you are facing, you will feel complete. But not yet. Between now and then, you will need to drop even this mask. When you become willing to give up hiding behind your spiritual identity, you will at last find the off-ramp from the repetitive cycling through life stages as you advance to the next stage of development: *Dismantling Your Masks*.

Dismantling Your Masks

B Y THE TIME YOU GET TO Stage 6, you will be less and less able to rationalize away the contributions you've inadvertently made that caused your mask to crack, less able to deny your unproductive attempts to place the blame for them on others or transcend the truth in a faux bolt for freedom. Facilitating this deconstruction, asking the question "why?" proves to be an effective tool for dismantling the masks that are already beyond repair. Transiting through the previous life stages to have made it this far, you have already taken one turn too many playing victim or savior. You already realize there must be more than exposing, evading, fixing, or punishing others, even if they have done you legitimate harm. There must also be more than attempting to break free by simply performing in knee-jerk reaction to all that you wish to reject or denying the whole mess entirely. You'll know you're in the sixth stage of development when you begin asking questions— *Why is this happening? Why do I try to do everything right, but it's never enough? Why do I keep making the same bad choices? Why is it that, no matter how hard I try, the experience of life I feel I deserve continues to elude me?*—and the answer is not somebody else's name.

Starting to ask yourself questions like these is unlikely to feel like progress, but rather as the path to falling apart that it truly is. You are letting go of your defenses, key aspects of your identity, and your go-to places of refuge. You may sense you are being called to go deeper, that there is something more deserving of you hidden beneath all the crumbling masks. But in order for you to get to it, you will have to face up to your most deeply hidden fears about yourself. When crisis hits, be it illness, the loss of someone who has been important to you, environmental disaster, or pandemic, all your defenses come tumbling down. Suddenly, you have no place to hide from yourself. Particularly problematical, even you no longer buy the old stories you've been telling yourself.

It is the hallmark of Stage 6 to feel that you are slipping backwards, not knowing why, after all these years invested in the belief that you were making something of yourself, it has amounted to so little. But there was a good reason that you held onto your masks for so long. Few are brave enough to let the entire personality project crumble to pieces earlier in life, and it is for the best, or at least inevitable, that you didn't. In fact, even flawed masks have their uses and are necessary to provide sufficient cover to allow you to engage in the world long enough to build not only a persona—but a life. You take up a career, find a mate, start a family, or whatever your own personal combination of constructed stepping stones that allows you some degree of safe passage through the chaos of human existence.

As do we all, I had to become "a somebody" in order to override the regressive power of my original wound and kick-start my life. If you are to survive, there is no alternative.

Subsequently, every life stage through which you've transited to the present moment has been in service of preparing you to face your wound, break through its limitations, embrace the truth of who you really are, and free your authentic self. In his insightful book *Recovery: The Sacred Art*, Rabbi Rami Shapiro reminds us of a story about Ram Dass who, while at the peak of his life as a spiritual master, suffered a severe stroke that left him with expressive aphasia and partial paralysis on his right side. In an instant, he was thrust from the mountaintop to the pit. Speaking of this experience years later, only partially recovered physically but evolved spiritually, Ram Dass shared that he received the guru's message that, with all his notoriety and even his good works, he was "no one special and had attained nothing of value." Only when the light can get in through the cracks in our masks are we able, in the words of Shapiro, to "see the truth of who we are and how distant we are from who we can become." Only then can we aspire to the stage of development Ram Dass came to value most: to become "a nobody." This developmental process comprises the heart of the human journey: not only the story of your life, but its very meaning. The making of an old soul takes place over the span of not years, but decades, and in Stage 6, you still have many stages to go.

Aspiring to become a nobody does not feel like something you are choosing for yourself. In fact, you are likely to feel that you've been singled out by fate as the only one who has ever been so unjustly treated. En route to the cemetery the day of my big reveal, I believed that Covid had, in some way I couldn't quite grasp, exposed me as having fallen short. Even so, I had already been having a harder and harder time denying that I wasn't the only one feeling this way. In my dual roles as host of the global Sage-ing International Book Club and member of an intimate dream group that met on Zoom throughout the pandemic, I became privy to the stories of my peers in real time. A yoga instructor in Russia. A seamstress in Israel. A spiritual counselor in Italy. A midwife in Tennessee. All of us, all over the world, were in lockdown. The questions that arose from the communal ethos transcended and embraced our particular time and place. And we are not the first generation to grow old in perilous times. In the words of Florida Scott-Maxwell, who wrote her classic about aging, *The Measure of My Days*, 50 years ago at the age of 86: "In hot rebellion we cry silently—'I have lived my life, haven't I? What more is expected of me?'" The primal wound—fear of separation, of abandonment, of betrayal—gets triggered over and over again. Over the first year of pandemic, we huddled, sheltering in place alone, virtually, or in shrinking pods, learning that we were not each the only one who, despite a lifetime dedicated to psychological and spiritual practice, had been exposed as wanting.

But shadow work has pitfalls of its own. There can be a thin line indeed between truth-telling and self-pity. If left to your own devices, you can all too easily sludge down into a quagmire of remorse, believing that you are the only one to have arrived at this advanced stage of life who has not yet figured it all out. In fact, at your first pass at life review, you are far more likely to retell old stories driven by your original wound, masquerading as sincere introspection, than to see the greater truth of who you are, where you've come from, where you actually do bear responsibility. Not all regret is merited, and it is equally important to identify those places and times when you have put yourself on trial falsely accused. But whatever the tremulous balance between introspection and remorse, attempting to answer the question *Why is this happening and what is my part in it?* is unsettling at best.

Regret will call to you, luring you backwards toward the comfort of old, familiar patterns, even as you are now so fully aware of the unintended consequences they bear. You are tempted to regress because you are already feeling the flames of imminent danger licking at your heels should you proceed with the dismantling. You are not yet sure enough if you can find it in you to give up your places of refuge because you do not know if, without your elaborate protections, you will survive. The truth is, you really *don't* know. But in your heart, and despite appearances to the contrary, you intuit that it is too late to resist the urge for growth that is compelling you to dust yourself off and answer the call. On paper, this sounds like something you want to do, something you are willing to commit to doing. But I warn you, answering the call will be beyond your ability. Your willpower will fail you. And even your hard-won faith that served you so well under fairer skies will falter. If and when you do respond, it will be because of *something more*, not of your own doing. This traditional story drawn from mystical traditions says it all.

A woman was taking a hike on a mountaintop when she slipped on a rock. Saving herself temporarily from a precipitous fall, she grabbed onto the overhanging branch of a tree. Then, hanging on for dear life, she heard a crack.

This woman hadn't prayed for quite some time, but thought this was as good a time as any to begin.

"God, are you up there?"

"Yes, my child," God replied. "What can I do for you?"

"God, help me. Tell me what to do!" she cried.

"You really want to know?"

The branch cracked a little more.

"Yes, God. Tell me!"

There was a moment's silence. Then God answered her.

"Let go of the branch."

"Let go of the branch?"

"Yes, my child. Let go of the branch."

There was another moment's silence, and then the woman spoke. "Is there anyone else up there?"

Hope has brought you this far, manifesting in the sense of *something more* that has and will be with you always. But for now, it is hopelessness that will serve you best—allowing the personality project to crumble the rest of the way, taking not only the image you hold of yourself as a psychologically and spiritually evolved person, but hope along with it. In Stage 6, even hopelessness has the potential to be put in service of increased consciousness, accelerating the pace of your journey through the culminating life stages that lie just ahead. You may not realize it at the time, but dismantling the personality project signifies the end not only of the story your wound has been telling you all your life, but of your victimhood.

Just when things appear to be at their bleakest, you will be fast approaching a turning point in your journey toward the *Making of an Old Soul*. The shift will come when you least expect it, at the exact moment you are feeling least worthy, least powerful, and least capable. And if you are brave enough to let it, it will break you.

The Void

YOU HAVE ANSWERED THE SUMMONS that has brought you to Stage 7, the culmination of the first part of your journey through the 11 stages that encompass the making of an old soul. Here, willpower is useless. You find yourself in the phase in your journey through the arc of life that signifies the successful dismantling of your personality project. But are you happy about this?

Some years ago, I was invited by the American Society of Aging to present about spirituality and aging alongside keynoter Jane Marie Thibault. Beforehand, we had the chance to compare notes about life-threatening illnesses we had suffered. Mine was well in the past, but Jane's encounter with mortality was fresh in her mind. Her words to the rapt audience that day resonated deeply. "Do you wish to persevere pridefully into the old life? Of course you do: the old life was a good life, but it is no longer available to you. It has been carried away irreversibly." Jane Marie, who has served as chaplain to the monks at Thomas Merton's monastery, Gethsemani, found she could not look forward until she'd taken the time to mourn: "To say Kaddish for the me who was . . . and would never be again."

And what is this place shrouded in shadows—the fearsome inevitability that you have worked so hard to avoid all your life? You'll know what it is in when you're in it: a dark and vast place, a bottomless pit, devoid of hope. You will feel listless, adrift, lost—but only when you aren't consumed by anxiety, regret, and grief. When you are in the place mystics describe as a void, you feel for all the world that you are the only one to have ever been in it. Listen to these words from the Psalms and see if they don't sound like they could have arisen from your own broken heart.

> *O Lord, God of my salvation,*
> *I have cried day and night before thee;*
> *Let my prayer come before thee; incline thine ear unto*
> *my cry;*
> *For my soul is full of troubles: and my life draweth nigh*
> *into the grave.*
> *I am counted with them that go down into the pit; I am*
> *as a man that hath no strength . . .*
> *Thou hast laid me in the lowest pit, in darkness, in*
> *the deep.*

There are archetypal forces, transcending the particulars of time and place, pulling you into the shadows as the chaos of life and whatever the times conspire to break you with. As the English writer Katherine Mansfield wrote in her private journal in 1923: "There is no limit to human suffering. When one thinks: 'Now I have touched the bottom of the sea—now I can go no deeper,' one goes deeper. And so it is forever . . . .What must one do? There is no question of what is called 'passing beyond it.' This is false. One must submit. Do not resist. Take it.

Be overwhelmed. Accept it fully. Make it a part of life . . . .The present agony will pass—if it doesn't kill."

These accounts of pain have withstood the test of time not because they are the words of losers who let life do them in, but because they are the courageous cries of vital spirits asserting themselves, willing to engage with the biggest questions of meaning and to struggle with God's very essence. Rejecting simplistic answers, overworked explanations, and rationalized defenses, these are the ones who let go of the branch, not knowing if they were going to hit bottom and, if they did, whether they would live or die. Their words, and the testimony of the many brave elders who have come before us, call out to each of us en route to the world of old souls, that feelings of despair are not yours alone but belong to all times and ages.

As we discussed in Stage 1, we are inheritors of human nature and largely predetermined responses to archetypal forces built into the DNA of our very being. Viewing us through this lens, Carl Jung writes that even "a creative person has little power over his own life. He is not free . . . ." And yet, little power is not no power. While at our best, we will struggle against triggers that tug us back toward habitual unconscious patterns all of our lives; the difference between enduring the shadows of unnamed dread versus living in as awakened a state as humanly possible is the degree of consciousness one succeeds in commandeering. "We are imperfect and dependent, but we have the freedom to choose—to the degree things become made conscious . . ." writes Jung. In fact, the more we become aware of those aspects of our patterning that come from the collective unconscious, the more freedom we will have in our lives to make meaning. We do so by devoting ourselves, as did Jung, to creating "more and more consciousness."

Knowing this, however, does not make your experience of falling into the void any less lonely or personal. Nor, at the time, does plummeting into the void feel like a choice. But nevertheless, your descent pays testimony to the courage it has taken for you to let go of the familiar because you know there's more to life than you've yet experienced, and you are willing to do whatever it takes, whatever the cost. Thomas Merton in *The Silent Life* describes one who has allowed life's challenges to shatter the last of his masks: "He can peacefully accept that when his false ideas of himself are gone he has practically nothing else left. But then he is ready for the encounters with reality: The Truth and the Holiness of God, which he must learn to confront in the depths of his own nothingness."

To take a stand for yourself against all evidence is often painful and, sometimes, nearly more pain than we can bear. But for those of us who persist against the odds, this is pain of a higher order. Spiritual teachers from many ages, faiths, and perspectives view the pain that results from both internal and external crisis not as a bad thing to be avoided but as a necessary instigator of spiritual growth. This spiritual interpretation of pain has many names. St. John of the Cross, in the 15th century, called it the *dark night of the soul.* The Kabala describes such a place as *Ein Sof* and, in some schools of Tibetan Buddhism, *bardo.* Anthropologists and scholars in the field of ritual studies call it *liminality.* However one refers to it, one experiences it as the discomforting period, unformed and unsettling, that comes between what was and what's next. Psychologists inform us that crisis is not built into the fabric of the actual events themselves. Rather, crisis occurs "when our theories about ourselves in relation to the outside world go fundamentally wrong," explains author Glenys Parry: "It is as if your front door, one day, instead of opening when you turned the key, gave you an electric shock." Rami Shapiro comments that when someone—like Ram Dass, struck out of the blue by a debilitating stroke—hits bottom with such force, "there is no opportunity for denial, no room for ego, no option for anything but a radically humble cry for help."

It is the dissonance between our expectations and our outcomes, both in regard to what we expect of the world, but also, and more to the point, what we expect of ourselves, that causes the pain—not the outcomes alone. Foremost among our expectations is the belief that pain is something to be avoided at all costs: that it is bad for you. While our culture tends to call surrendering to pain "apathy," the Greek root for apathy actually means the avoidance, not the experience, of suffering. Transformation begins the moment you admit that the precipitous event that ultimately took you under has outstripped your capacity to manage the world to your satisfaction, and that you are out of tricks. When you stop trying to force your will upon the world, you accept the limits to your power.

Nothing is more effective than crisis for emptying your bag of tricks. Crisis foils your expectations, shakes you out of the false security of the status quo, and carries the potential to wake you up not only to your own limitations but to the truth about reality. There have been many who have endured the journey and survived to tell the tale, like Ram Dass, Thibault and Scott-Maxwell. Not only did they survive, but they emerged more vital, more integrated, more connected to life's possibilities, not despite of but because of having undergone catastrophe. The void is, after all, the place where the status quo has the least grip on you, and where you are most able to let go of old structures, illusions, and outgrown ways of being. It is in the void that you are most likely to shed the beliefs that once circumscribed the meaning in your life and to take up what had never before occurred to you, the unpremeditated and radically new.

Pema Chodron illustrates this with the story of Milarepa, one of the holders of the Kagyii lineage of Tibetan Buddhism. Milarepa was a hermit, passing many years alone trying to perfect himself by meditating in the caves of Tibet. One night he returned to his cave after gathering firewood, only to discover that demons had taken over his abode. A demon was reading Milarepa's book; one was sleeping on his bed. They were all over the place. Hoping to take control of the situation, Milarepa came up with an idea. He would teach them about spirituality. He found a seat higher than theirs and began to lecture about compassion. The demons simply ignored him. Then Milarepa got really angry and charged at them, but they simply laughed at him. Finally, he gave up, sitting down on the floor of the cave with them, surrendering to the difficult fact that, since he could do nothing to either change or get rid of them, they might as well learn to live together.

At that moment, they left—all except one. Recognizing the need for total surrender, Milarepa arrived at his last resort. He walked over and put himself right into the mouth of the demon. He literally fed himself to what he had been fearing most. At that moment, the demon departed, leaving Milarepa alone but transformed. He had finally run out of tricks and had become willing to pay the price more and more consciousness extracts from even the most spiritually committed. Pema Chodron writes: "Instead of transcending the suffering of all creatures, we move toward the turbulence and doubt. We jump into it. We slide into it. We tiptoe into it. We move toward it however we can . . . . With us move millions of others, our companions in awakening from fear. At the bottom we discover water, the healing water of bodhichitta. Right down there in the thick of things, we discover the love that will not die."

The progression through life depends on this cycle of destruction and renewal, taking its model from what humanity has observed since the dawn of time: Nature privileges spirals and cycles over sticks and linear trajectories. The seasons, the phases of the moon, the cycle of life. This is the essence of life's meaning as embodied in the *I Ching*, the ancient Chinese *Book of Changes*. At any given point, certain aspects of our lives are falling away, new aspects birthing. This disruption and renewal is what characterizes our progress through life stages, and not only in the purview of mystics. As Nobel Prize-winning chemist Ilya Prigogine postulated, in healthy organisms there is a necessary period of stasis after deconstruction that he refers to as "the theory of dissipative structures." Utilizing the scientific method, Prigogine theorized that people, things, and events are involved in a continuous exchange of energy, impacting one another on an ongoing basis. When something disturbs or upsets the system, the components have the capacity to reorganize into a higher order. When applied to cognitive function, it is the impact of new information, pleasant or not, that causes the spontaneous realignment of neural relationships into the more evolved hierarchy of thought we think of as "breakthrough," "insight," or "revelation."

The moment you come to understand that your pain is not necessarily about what's wrong with you but rather about that which yearns to grow larger, the very forces that have been pushing you from behind give way, and when the night is darkest, you catch a glimmer of what had previously been hidden in plain sight: that powerlessness is also freedom. In psychological terms, this turn toward increased consciousness is known as "preparation." Rather than resist the pain, you use it as a point of entry into your deeper consciousness, where progress is possible.

One who willingly chose descent was Jacob, son of Isaac. You recall the story from the Hebrew scriptures about Jacob's deception of his father, Isaac. Jacob used a sheepskin to simulate the hair on his brother Esau's arm in order to steal his brother's blessing from his blind and trusting father. Upon this fraudulent foundation, Jacob climbed the ladder of success, continuing to play his role in the ways of the world, taking turns being deceived by others and defrauding them right back. By the peak of his life, he had acquired a large, attractive family, wealth, position, and not just one wife but two. Far away from the discomforting memory of his father and Esau, he looked to the world as if he had it all. But there was something missing from his life that, despite all his clever manipulations, had continued to elude him.

As so often happens in stories of spiritual heroism, when you become willing to engage in struggles worthy of yourself, the path forward can be found. For Jacob, the yearning for rectification was to be answered in a place of deep descent, the Jabbok River. Jacob had packed up his formidable possessions and embarked on what he hoped would be a journey toward reconciliation with Esau. By the time the descent into the river gorge was complete, it was deepest night. Something prompted Jacob to send his caravan across the river to the distant shore while he remained behind, alone in the dark. No family or wives to distract him. No heads of cattle to count. On his own, stripped of his trappings and masks, he was suddenly confronted by a presence: an unnamed spirit who came to wrestle with him in the shadows. All night long, he struggled with his deceit, his desire to dominate, his shame and his guilt, manifesting in the form of this divine being. He wrestled with the very imperfection of his own humanity: that painful discrepancy between how one hopes one is being perceived by others and the flawed version of reality one fears is the truth.

Eventually the sun rose. The struggle ended, but not before Jacob understood how much his decision to do whatever it would take to awaken spiritually would cost him. He who for so long had sought only to stride triumphant over others had been rendered lame, exhausted, helpless, and begging the Divine for a blessing: a way forward. The crux of his redemption, however, was not about Jacob asking what God would or would not deliver to him, but rather his having been willing to put it all on the line and to literally be broken the rest of the way. For Jacob, the price he paid for more and more consciousness was steep indeed. In the end, he did receive God's blessing and went on to reconcile with his brother, who forgave and embraced him. But at the same time, he was permanently damaged. The limp that was to become his only way forward served as an ongoing reminder of the price he had paid for freedom.

As you progress through the arc of life, your newfound humility will continue emptying you of the last vestiges of your will to power. And here the void reveals its true nature: not as punishment, not as an ending, not even as culmination. But a pause—a place of resting where the push of your original wound loosens its grip and you are made ready for a transformation so profound it leaves even the mystics breathless. God blessed Jacob with what Ram Dass refers to as "fierce grace": coming to see and make peace with the whole truth about yourself, all the while accepting that there will always be a discrepancy between your ideals and your reality. Jacob's experience reminds you that you may deceive others, make mistakes, get your values turned upside down, but only when you become willing to face up to and rectify what you can no longer avoid do you become a candidate for the fulfillment of life's promise. The Jewish mystics call this turn toward the good *teshuva* and the individual willing to engage in this holy struggle a *tzaddik*, a righteous soul.

The freedom of powerlessness comes not out of your achievements, but out of laying down the burden of sustaining the illusion of who you had thought yourself to be, ending your exhausting struggle to maintain control, and ceasing to pretend that you have achieved any semblance of life mastery. The life review that you undertook spontaneously in Stage 6, *Dismantling Your Masks,* was necessary for you to understand how the arc of your life thus far had been destined from the first to push you over the edge into the void. Reviewing all the life stages through which you've progressed, you can see now the logic and inevitability of how your life played out over time, from the pain that accompanied your very first intake of breath on. You made many choices along the way that brought you to Stage 7, some consciously, many more unconsciously. And now you are once again at a crossroads with a new choice to make: *Will you choose despair, or will you choose freedom?* Making the choice for freedom over despair is not an action step—it's a prayer. It is the nobodyness of a Ram Dass and the nothingness of a Merton.

Recalling Thibault's call to Kaddish, I was inspired to dig out the journals I'd been keeping at the time of my diagnosis of breast cancer 25 years ago, capturing the essence of what the void asks of you: "There are those times in our lives when the pain is so great, it is enough to remind yourself to just keep breathing. I trust that, in time, I will discover whether or not there is inherent meaning in what is happening to me. But I also realize that to short-circuit, circumvent, or deny my pain by pretending I believe that this is some kind of gift when I clearly do not is to trivialize and degrade both myself and the Divine. Rather, I find it challenge enough simply to stay sufficiently alert to wrestle with the real questions underlying my faltering faith. Sometimes, all we can do is feel. And thankfully, it is enough."

In the end, it is only your honest tears that prove to be strong enough to dissipate the forces that have been pushing you from behind from birth, setting you free. This is life's promise to you—a new way of being in the world calling out to you. And so it is we are made ready to turn the page to the culminating life stages of *The Making of an Old Soul* and the promise of arrival.

Conscious Aging

YOU HAVE ARRIVED at a new life stage, crying for help. But while you experience yourself as having hit bottom, Conscious Aging is the developmental stage that allows you to come to understand that letting yourself be cracked to the core represents not only an abject state of giving up, but the beginning of retrieval, rectification, and healing. Central to the making of old souls is this summons to awaken from collusion with our shadows and face them head on. When everything falls apart, that is where we are most able to make significant changes in our lives. This place of collapse, in fact, is where the making of an old soul begins in earnest. Eventually we emerge from the darkness, glad for every percentage point we manage to wrest from our unconscious defenses. Much of this growing self-knowledge—the ongoing shedding of illusions and the confrontation with the truth—continues to be painful but can also provide fertile ground for surprises.

For instance, there were all the unexpected twists and turns taken by my neighbor Shelly, shortly after turning 80. We were brought together by our dogs, instant friends who could not pass one another on the neighborhood sidewalk without extended sniffs, nose rubs, and friendly competition for the best shrub. Over the years, Shelly and I deepened our own friendship, stopping at walk's end for a glass of wine at one of our cherished houses, sharing hopes for our adult sons and daughters and our young grandchildren, talking about our projects, and solving the problems of the world while the dogs romped in the garden. A retired actress who was once considered Hollywood royalty, Shelly was no stranger to the losses associated with age. She inspired me with her graceful acceptance of her dramatically altered status in life. But there came a day when I began noticing subtle changes. At first, Shelly would be surprised when I showed up at her door at the scheduled time. Then there was the time she couldn't remember my dogs' names. Not long after that, she was diagnosed with early stage dementia. The decline was gradual but steady, and while I thought I was as ready as any friend could be to face the uncertainties of the future together, it turned out I was completely unprepared for what happened next.

It was a sunny day when the dogs and I stood on her front stoop waiting for Shelly to open the door. The door opened a crack, and an unfriendly middle-aged woman peeked out. From Shelly's descriptions, I recognized this stranger as her daughter, a downtown lawyer who treated Shelly more as babysitter to her son than beloved mother to herself. In clipped tones, Karen informed me that her mother had been moved to a facility, the dogs were being fostered, and the children would be putting the house up for sale. She refused to provide me with contact information, so I was left on my own to fret, feeling as worried as I was helpless.

The *For Sale* sign went up quickly and weeks passed with no word from Shelly. Until, one day, there came a knock on my door. There was Shelly, her dogs at the end of their leashes, all

66

of them wild with excitement. Karen had underestimated her mom, and quite frankly, Shelly hadn't known she had it in her. But after several weeks at the institution, she found an ally on the staff who helped her hire a lawyer. That very day, she called a taxi, packed up the one box of belongings her daughter had allowed her to take from the house, and went home. With the support of the lawyer and home health, Shelly got not only her dogs back but her life.

Shelly is a realist, and knows that there will come a time when she may not be able to take adequate care of herself, let alone her dogs. She wishes her daughter would apologize or at least talk to her again, and if nothing else, allow her to see her grandchild. But having been through this untimely dress rehearsal, she is determined to pay the price of staying the course in her own home as long as possible, grateful to have the means to pay for adequate care. And meanwhile, when I show up at her door, and she forgets I was coming, we both have a good laugh and she grabs her jacket.

There is plenty of room in all this for forgiveness and compassion—not only for others and the world, but for ourselves. We do what we can to rectify the past, try to do better in the present, and hope that, in the wisdom of time, some greater good will come from whatever wreckage we have inadvertently left behind. By answering the questions posed to us by fate, we discover that things are not always what they seem—often not as bright and shiny as we'd hoped for but sometimes bearing the most unexpected and precious gifts, more than we'd ever imagined for ourselves: recognition of the dependable heart that had been beating beneath it all from the first. Even when we're triggered or suffering, we can come to trust that sooner or later we will do what we can to bring more consciousness into a world that needs an antidote to unconsciousness on every level, from the intensely personal to the pervasive global, now more than ever.

This sounds big and important—and it can be. It can even be transcendent: angels descending from heaven and lifting us up. But an advance in consciousness can also start very small. After our sweet Maltese, Sammy, the oldest of our pack of dogs, went blind in one eye, it was as if his defenses melted away and all that was left of him was a puddle of love. No, not always angels descending but something just as miraculous. "Did Sammy's tail always do that?" I asked Dan the other day. We'd been fostering Sammy for over four years for the Old Friends Senior Dog Sanctuary and thought we knew every one of his charming quirks. But within an hour of each other, Dan and I had witnessed the same thing. Every time he spotted us with his one good eye, his nondescript nub of a tail—so small and tucked down we hadn't previously taken conscious note of it—would rise up into a grand curl as perfect as a wave at Waimea Bay. And then it would wag. This was a sight so glorious I could not help weeping for joy. And not just for the love that poured forth from a dog that one could easily think of as broken, but that we did not know for sure whether, until we were faced with the precious fragility of his life, we just hadn't noticed. And while what you encounter at this life stage can't promise to put everything back the way it was or deliver on your expectations for a particular future, it is necessary for the co-creation of the optimal environment for spiritual quickening to transpire.

Situated at the intersection of psychology, religion, mysticism, and spiritual recovery, Conscious Aging draws from all of those and more for both inspiration and restorative modalities, as applied particularly to the aging process. This is the pivotal life stage during which increased consciousness and intention can at last trump reliance upon instinct, inevitability, and external forces. There is efficiency to the practice of Conscious Aging, in which everything that took place throughout the arc of your life can be understood to have happened for a purpose. This profound shift in perspective begins the moment when, even in the pit of despair, you catch yourself turning your eyes upwards to a Power greater than yourself, whether to ask for help or in rebuke. With this spontaneous and poignantly guileless act, you have arrived at the culminating stages of spiritual development, what the "Anonymous" programs prescribe as the first of the 12 Steps of Recovery, having "admitted we were powerless— that our lives had become unmanageable."

Earlier, we saw this in Jacob as he wrestled all night on the banks of the Jabbok River and in Ram Dass as he lay paralyzed by a stroke. As Kathleen Dowling Singh wrote in *The Grace in Aging,* people come to deeper consciousness only by intentional struggles with contradictions, conflicts, inner confusions, and perceived failures: "We may have thought of the spiritual path as all-glorious, like a rose-tinged, many-petaled lotus opening into unimaginable radiance. Maybe that's so, but . . . there will be a lot of bugs and spiders and slugs that will scurry out of their hiding places in the lotus petals before those petals are fully opened . . . .Although it leads to greater and greater ease, the spiritual path is not all easy. It is, however, doable by any of us ordinary human beings, with wise effort and clear intention." Doable, yes, and Conscious Aging is the life stage whose defining characteristic is the utilization of specific tools and techniques that allow you to make increasingly conscious choices regarding your pace of advancement. But it does not mean you won't grieve your losses, not the least of which is the erosion of your illusion of power. In this, growing older has an advantage and, in the sequence of the life stages, represents an order, an internal logic, and a progression that has led author and mystic John C. Robinson to refer to aging as "evolution in slow motion."

When it comes to transiting into and through Stage 8, the losses that come about with advancing age turn out to be the very means to advancement. Those of us who have attended so many retreats in order to loosen ego's grip on us need now only look in the mirror to feel humbled. Your ambition to make something of yourself, which drove you relentlessly all your life, now sits at your feet like an old dog that has lost its bite. You may already recycle, purchase your clothes at thrift shops, and drive a Prius, but it is far easier to become less materialistic when you have downsized to a room in your daughter's house. Writes Robinson in *The Three Secrets of Aging:* "As we move into old age, our familiar identity loses its importance. It is fading or long gone. We also begin to lose interest in thought, itself—our thoughts no longer seem so important and seem to disappear more quickly, along with all the underlying ideas that structure our conventional understanding of identity, time, reality, and story."

You will recall having undertaken spontaneous self-reflection in an earlier life stage when at the dawn of self-awareness you first began asking "why." But at that time, still attempting to exercise what little power you thought you had left in you, chances are that you mistook serious introspection for self-rebuke and remorse. Having arrived at Stage 8, you have the opportunity to revisit this task from the more advanced stage of psychological and spiritual development Conscious Aging represents. Here, the charge is to confront and then clear away the debris of regret, victimhood, blame, self-doubt, and all manner of misunderstanding from your path.

If you are unsure how to proceed, the 12-step program, with its step-by-step guidance, can lead you through the process from powerlessness to spiritual awakening. While there is no 12-step program designed to overcome your addiction to youth and power, there are 52 subjects that have adapted recovery principles originally aimed toward alcoholism to their own purposes. From an addiction to clutter to codependency, in recovery rooms you may find not only principles but fellow travelers who understand what you're going through, walking with you every step of the way. You can also find support and guidance in therapy, spiritual retreats, even confession. Being in community helps, and many of us who see ourselves as fellow seekers are somehow finding our way to one another, breaking up the isolation and negative stereotypes associated with growing older. Conscious Aging is not just a life stage, it's a movement, and small gatherings, like the book club I cohost for Sage-ing International, have started meeting in person and online around the world. While the Conscious Aging movement embraces renegade visionaries from a wide range of disciplines and spiritual traditions, it is no accident that it was mystics like Schachter-Shalomi and Ram Dass, many with academic credentials, who got it going. But whatever the philosophy, tools, and modalities, individuals who identify with the notion of Conscious Aging share the revolutionary notion of older age as a life stage with meaning, task, and purpose of its own.

What is this task? Rami Shapiro finds the words in Vipassana: to commit to "a nonjudgmental encounter with reality." You have already learned that you have no power over others, especially those who trigger you. But this is just the low-hanging fruit. Using whatever degree of consciousness you can bring to bear on self-awareness, you soon learn that the only things you have ever had control over are your ability to tell the truth, to rectify whatever wrongs you have done in the past, to make better choices going forward, and to ask for help from the Divine, as do all who aspire to become old souls, because no one can do even this much without the help of something more. Allowing this stage to evolve over time will be the central task of your journey through Conscious Aging as you become more accustomed to—and less afraid of—productive pain. You may have questions, disappointments, concerns, and confusion about how you got to the age you are, only to feel that you have been so wrong about so many things. But if you submit whatever is troubling you to conscious reflection, you will recognize the opportunity to deepen your understanding of the circumstances into which you were born and a lifetime of choices—some good, some not so much—holding the potential for you to accept the entire arc of your life thus far and to move on.

If this sounds like a tall order, the *Serenity Prayer*, written by American theologian Reinhold Niebuhr in 1943, spells it out in just 25 words. "God, grant me the serenity to accept the things I cannot change; courage to change the things I can; and wisdom to know the difference." As Joan Chittiser sums up: "I must surrender to the final truth: She did not love me. They do not want me. What I want is not possible. And, hardest to bear of all, all arguments to the contrary are useless . . . .Life as I had fantasized it is ended. What is left is the spiritual obligation to accept reality so that the spiritual life can really happen in me."

One changes what one can and accepts what one cannot. Neither option is what you'd hoped to ever have to do. But this is not the hard part. The most challenging aspect of the *Serenity Prayer* is hidden in plain sight: *The wisdom to know the difference*. If you think you are already certain about your ability to determine which is yours to do in any given situation, ask yourself: *How can I be sure if my unwillingness to judge another is tolerance or cowardice? Is my love unconditional or am I hoping to get something in return out of the deal, even something as admirable as peace of mind?* These are issues you may struggle with at many ages and life stages, and how you answer contributes to the building of character. But aging, compounded by added responsibilities and accumulating losses, has its own exigent questions. *Do I keep mom on dialysis or let her go? How many times do I pay my granddaughter's electric bill? Do I stay in the community where I have put down my roots or follow my adult children to their new jobs in cities far away?* Discerning what is yours to fight for or whether you are being called to let go is not something you can order up on demand.

Even Ram Dass, before his stroke, had a hard time figuring out what to accept versus what to change. In his book, *Still Here*, Ram Dass tells a story about the time when, at the age of 63, he'd been invited to speak before an audience of thousands in Denver. Rather than walk up the steps to the podium, he decided to show off by leaping straight to the stage. He miscalculated his strength and the trajectory, and took a painful fall. Even then he didn't want to lose face, so he gave his speech with blood dripping down his leg. In retrospect, he wishes he had had the humility to "act his age," accepting his limitations, and excuse himself for the brief time it would have taken to tend to his wound properly. Ram Dass learned valuable life lessons from this embarrassing episode—adding to the bank of his spiritual resources he would have to draw upon when three years later, he suffered his stroke. He writes that, before his paralysis, he thought the losses associated with age were his to change—to overcome with an act of will in service of his ego. But he came to realize that he had been prone to overestimating his powers. "Or perhaps, I was simply more arrogant. In any case, it is fascinating now to discover that the embarrassment I felt over getting older has nearly disappeared with my physical disability. Back then, I was worried about not looking fit. Since the stroke I have been wheelchair-bound . . . . This was much harder to take at the beginning. It gets easier as the Ego lets go of its concerns." While Ram Dass hoped that, when he accepted the reality of his aging after his humiliating fall, he was done fooling himself, it was to be three more years before he stopped trying to change things and accepted reality as it is.

Shaking one's addiction to the will to control is a tricky business, and questions that come in service of sincere spiritual aspiration can still seduce and mislead you. Previously, we discussed faux spirituality as just a fancier mask for arrogance offering the illusion of life mastery. Now, in Stage 8, faux spirituality of a higher order arises again, this time feigning the mask of humility. *If only I humble myself enough; if only I stop trying to fix others good enough; if only I can make sufficient amends; if only I surrender enough, I can make things right for me, you, and the world.* This is not freedom. This is your final mask.

The irony is that this last gasp of power can come dressed up as everything that psycho-spiritual maturity seems to ask of us: humility, surrender, acceptance. But in Stage 8, the appearance of these very attributes turns against you because they come not in the name of the healing of your original wound, but in service to it. You'll know that you are still holding on to this last remnant of the illusion of control when you secretly harbor the sense that something is off and that, despite having made amends, rectifying what you can and accepting the rest, you believe you should be able to do something more about it. This urge to be spiritual enough is the hardest to crack—perfectionism, martyrdom, altruism, and their particularly insidious unintended consequence: the belief in your eternal need for self-improvement. If you are not sure whether you qualify, ask yourself if you can apologize sincerely one time, make appropriate amends, and know you've done enough? Or are you walking the earth wearing a hair shirt, still begging forgiveness for the affair you had 40 years ago or parenting errors you made when your children were young? It may look good to you and to others to aim to become a penitent, a martyr, or even the personification of your best possible self, but as long as you hold the belief that your efforts to improve yourself will consequently fix, save, cure, help, or heal if not others, then your own life, you are not spiritually awakened. You are grandiose.

This last grasp at power will be only the latest in a long progression of the strategies you've attempted thus far—victimhood, rebellion, and now the incipient attempt to take personal responsibility—that are doomed to disappoint. This is because none addresses the true nature of the wound: the deeply held fear that your essential wrongness was the cause of the catastrophe of separation and everything that has resulted. Having read this far, you may well be coming to understand that what at least some of what you thought of as taking personal responsibility was actually not the remedy for character flaws but a flaw itself. But at the same time, we are not only our least desirable traits. If we tell the whole truth, the things we don't like about ourselves are not all of who we are, nor are the things we like least about the world all there is. One assumes there are things we like—even love—about ourselves, others, and the world as well. On the last page of Carl Jung's autobiography, the great psychologist writes: "I am astonished, disappointed, pleased with myself. I am distressed, depressed, rapturous. I am all these things at once, and cannot add up the sum. I am incapable of determining ultimate worth or worthlessness; I have no judgment about myself and my life. There is nothing I am quite sure about . . . ." Jung is as rapturous as he is deflated. And, too, when it comes to me and to all of us, it is, indeed, complicated.

Down the road, you will have the opportunity to revisit the attributes that comprise the heart of spiritual awakening, and the next time you meet up with them, they will deliver on their promise because you will be in a new place, and you will be ready. But in Stage 8, the thought has already dawned on you that you cannot make it on your own. Our best efforts will never be enough. We all need help. Turning over your will means you are giving up entirely—you are going to stop trying. No more clinging or strategizing. *Letting go and letting God* is not pretty, not gift-wrapped. On your own, you cannot will into being either change, acceptance, or even discernment. The only thing you can do is tell the truth—as much as you can bear, and then a bit more—and keep doing so relentlessly. When acceptance finally comes, this is not something you are doing for God. Rather, it is something God offers to you, but only when you have already surrendered. Writes Richard Rohr in *Breathing Under Water:* "God has trapped us all inside of certain grace and enclosed all things human in a constant need for mercy . . . . All we can do is keep out of the way, note, and weep over our defensive behaviors . . . and the presence that is surely the highest Power is then obvious, all-embracing and immediately effective." In discerning the difference between what he could change versus what he had to accept, Ram Dass's stroke forced him to face his worst fears and beg for mercy. But while there were painful losses, there were also unexpected gifts. The greatest blessing was the wearing away of the effects of his ego: the attachment to how others perceived him, to expectations about what kind of life he deserved, even to what he had thought was the meaning of life itself. As Ram Dass describes it: "Behind the machinations of our brilliant, undependable minds is an essence that is not conditional, a being that aging does not alter, to which nothing can be added, from which nothing is taken away . . . ."

It is time now to continue progressing through the arc of life in the direction of the dénouement which I have been promising from the beginning.

— STAGE 9 —

The Big Reveal

WELCOME TO THE THRESHOLD OF Stage 9, after you have spent significantly more time than anticipated transiting through Stage 8. Having read this far, you already know a great deal about the contents of the big reveal that flooded over me during my walk through the cemetery. But as I'm poised here on the edge of recounting the rest of what I came to understand that day, I have suddenly recalled that the big reveal was not my first mystical encounter with the meaning of the arc of life. But my previous encounter belonged to somebody else and I was only the witness.

Until this very moment, whenever I was asked about my mother's last words, I recounted the story I shared with you earlier, in which she ascribed my brother's absence to my "having sucked all the air out of the room." On this side of Stage 8, having done multiple moral inventories, I must acknowledge that, while there are good explanations for it, I have indeed sucked my fair share of air from more than one room. In this regard, I have rectified what I can and accepted the rest and that would have been that, but for the ice storm that for the South marked one year into the pandemic.

The big reveal took place on a balmy day in early spring a number of seasons ago. But this morning, when I sat down to write about it, I awoke to the biggest winter storm Nashville had experienced in years. Whatever wasn't blanketed with shimmering snow was glazed over with ice. This would have been dazzling except that a pipe burst overnight, dripping water through the kitchen floor onto a waterlogged black file box tucked into a shadowy corner of the basement. While Dan triaged the mess upstairs, I went down and opened the lid. Inside was the now watermarked journal I kept as I sat watch over my mother's final days. I peeled open the moist cover and found the story I remember. But I felt a chill run the length of my spine. These were not her last words. After my mother put the blame for my brother squarely and unfairly on me, I'd gone to the reception area and thought about leaving for good. But I returned and, drawing upon depths of compassion I did not know I had, took her surprisingly warm hand in mine. She turned her blind eyes in my direction and then, only then, did she speak her last words. "My beautiful, beautiful, beautiful, beautiful daughter. This is a big world and you're in it." Then she fell silent. But she didn't let go.

For a second, or was it minutes, our minds merged and her thoughts were my own. It was as if I were watching a movie with my eyes closed, but the images unfolded faster than I could ever have intended. There I am, crying for the breast that was never to be offered, a thousand more frames, then the moment Mom gets the family portrait she's commissioned back from the photography studio and realizes that from my explosion of curls to the grin on my face, everything about me at age four is too much. In a rush of images, determined trips to department stores, my little legs hurrying to keep up with her, leaping ahead to adolescence and endless arguments about my choice of friends, my clothes, and my selfish behavior, fast-forwarding to temporarily disowning me when I got engaged to someone outside our faith. I took it all in, reliving each shadowed moment with her. But then the lighting changed, and there I was back in childhood where she was now beaming from the front row of my first piano recital; now years later, buying my first published book to give to all the relatives; now freely sharing with my growing children the joy that she had withheld from me. And then the images stopped as suddenly as they started. In the wordless whisper of her final out-breath, I felt my mother ask me for forgiveness. And I gave it. In that moment, she released my hand and my eyes shot open. I saw the blanket on her chest fall and watched as the starched white hospital room burst into a field of white atoms and carbonated gold. I instinctively recognized this as the passing of her soul, and her final gift to me. We did not need to wait any longer to feel complete. She and I were enough. I was enough. This was enough. In the hours following, I recorded all of this in my journal, locked it in a black box, and stored it in the basement only to return immediately to the rut of my old story that stopped short of her true last words: back to the story that affirmed my victimhood rather than forgiveness.

In Stage 9, we can finally question the veracity of the stories our original wounds have been telling us: that we have been so wronged, so misunderstood, so unworthy. We can find the courage and the strength to break from the well-worn ruts of the past to see the whole truth about ourselves, others, and the world—accepting not just the shadows but the light. And we know, without having to change a single thing about our lives, that our prayers are being answered. This is what my mother experienced as she exhaled her last breath and what seekers yearn for throughout the arc of their lives: the final healing of the gap of original separation and all of its unintended consequences. But Mom's death was 20 years ago, and while I witnessed something miraculous, there were many more life stages to come before I was to have the answer underlying every seeker's question: *Is it possible to have this experience not at the end of life but with decades to spare?*

If life has proven that it can be counted upon for anything, it would be that the bar for mastery can always be raised—often when you're least expecting it. If you are a seeker, you recommit to continuing the work of Conscious Aging, putting in months or years of devoted practice, hoping you are getting somewhere. But then, inevitably, there comes a time when you've done everything in your power to make things right, rectified everything possible, and still find yourself wandering like a ghost through the wreckage of your life. What more could you have done? What is the missing piece? It is no accident that the day of my big reveal occurred in a deserted place consisting of rows upon rows of the dead: the only place of refuge where one could walk without a mask in a dangerously out-of-control world.

Moments after I'd set foot on cemetery lawn, random scenes from my life had begun flashing before my eyes. But this time, I was not simply witness to another's life review. The series of images jumped from as recently as this day's troubling events to painful memories that had not surfaced for decades. Our beloved dog Molly's death, still fresh and acute; the persistent look of disappointment in my mother's eyes; friends who'd disappeared without explanation; the shock of the diagnosis of breast cancer; the daily news relentlessly defining age as an underlying condition; row upon row of the dead, fallen for and against injustice that was not of their making just as bodies were piling up in hospital corridors and morgues only a mile away from where I stood.

Backlit by the unrelenting spotlight of the pandemic, it has become increasingly difficult for our generation to sweep dread under the rug. And as if it weren't wake-up call enough, the tragedy of Covid has triggered unprocessed emotions for the untimely and difficult deaths of so many on whom we had come to depend. We can't be good and determined enough to outrun the grim reaper (Ruth Bader Ginsburg). We can't be spiritual enough (Reb Zalman). Over the course of the last decades, I'd suffered the loss of my parents' entire generation of family members: aunts, uncles, and older cousins. Now I'd outlived mentors, spiritual directors, and tai chi instructors. With every phone call, I have been but one degree of separation from someone who lost a husband, a child, a dad. Dan lost his best friend and bandmate, Roger, then death reached its bony fingers into our home over the course of the pandemic over and over again, taking not only Molly, not only Sammy's eye, but then, even on this very day as I sit here trying to remember to breathe through my tears, the family dog we raised from puppyhood to old age, our precious Lucky, too. Each of these deaths has caught me off-guard, reminding me that intensity of love cannot be counted on to mitigate pain and suffering. Processing these difficult losses, I am that much more aware that our time on earth under the best of circumstances is limited, and more to the point, that even our spiritual resources are no guarantee that any of us can avoid doubts, pain, and suffering.

No one is more surprised than I to have been so unprepared to stare down death at this advanced age and stage of my life. The breast cancer diagnosis was decades ago. You would think that, having survived, my denial of death would have long ago been faced and broken. But I now realize that, as serious as it was, getting breast cancer while in my 40's was something from which I could at least hope to survive. But aging is not something from which any of us can ever hope to recover. The stakes have been raised as we age, our spiritual fantasies put to ever bigger tests. We wish we could turn the clock back to the time we truly believed that we would never have to face anything that could not be overcome by prayer, diligent work, and positive thinking. But aging has made the illusion of immortality impossible to maintain. And yet we try. Why?

Existential philosopher Rollo May and psychotherapist Irvin Yalom each contend that the dramas of aging that threaten to sweep us through the years beyond midlife are little more than stand-ins for what it is that is really bothering us. Anxiety about our adult children and grandchildren, for instance, may seem to be about whether they're fulfilling their potential. Of course, there is a degree of concern that is normal and natural when it comes to those we care for. But when there is an excessive expression of anxiety, especially when coupled with a misplaced sense of responsibility for their lives as adults, it is a signal to look deeper. Peel away your knee-jerk judgments and see if your concerns are, in fact, an antidote to your fear of death: the hope for immortality through your offspring. Anxieties about your financial future can be traced to similar roots. Do you cringe at the financial planner's question, "How long do you plan to live?" Or do you avoid the planning process entirely, knowing that this question of finite lifespan is too threatening to be addressed? Does your ambition to leave a lasting legacy stem from the sincere desire to make a difference or the anxious concern that otherwise you will be forgotten? Do you have trouble making choices, let alone commitments, because in doing so, you view your life as one of diminishing rather than expanding possibilities? Do you stay busy not because there's so much you want to do but because otherwise there's nothing to drown out the persistent sense that something's off? Our everyday anxieties keep us flailing at the surface of things, whipped here and there by deeper currents we do not even know have us in their grip.

And then, for me, there came the walk in the cemetery, when all the busyness and noise suddenly gave way and I saw how small I really am, how big the world. That being "a nobody" is not just a spiritual aspiration: it's the truth. At that moment, the entire arc of my life ran in reverse before my eyes. But this time, all made sense, nothing was left undone. In an in-flooding of expanded awareness, I saw that I had, indeed, worked long and hard to acknowledge and rectify every one of my unintended consequences, but that unconsciousness is not something you choose: not something you did "wrong." In that moment, I knew that I had been forgiven for every misstep subsequent to the original separation, which I finally saw was never my responsibility or under my control. In fact, the unconsciously held premise of my essential wrongness that had been driving me from birth was a fundamental misunderstanding.

You can't make amends for what is not yours to fix. Not for what is in your DNA; the archetypal forces; anybody else's choices; or the 96 percent of your brain scientists postulate is held unconsciously. Nor can you change how others feel about who you truly are when you become less willing to compromise, hide, or defend your true self. We are limited, finite, mortal, human. The entirety of this book that flooded into me came in service of this one simple message: that the original wound is universal and inevitable and that everything that subsequently unfolds throughout the 11 stages of our lives is not just personal. Once one has rectified all that one can, there is no more cause for compunction.

But there was more, for at the same time, not all of your unintended consequences are only creatures of the shadows in need of rectification. Goodness, kindness, generosity: these, too, can manifest spontaneously from depths you did not know you had. There is, as I have been saying from the very first page, *something more* at work in your life, whispering to you that, regardless of how bad things may appear at any given time, you are beloved unconditionally, eternally. Bad things do happen that are unfair, unjust, unkind. You may even unintentionally (or not) have played a role. But none of this has come about because there is something irredeemable about you.

That day in the cemetery, I could suddenly see my previously unconsciously held beliefs about life turned upside down. I recognized where I'd gotten stuck and the stories I'd wrongly taken to be the truth of myself, others, and the world. And at that moment, the force that had been pushing me from behind from birth loosened its grip and dissipated into a wisp. This persistent force that had been propelling me forward was gone, and at long last I came to rest. Liminality deepened into stasis: a state of equanimity. And then, with my next in-breath, when I was least expecting it: the pivot. Rays of hope that had been reaching out to me from my own future since the beginning, no more than filaments, revealed themselves to me. Like the rising sun, they grew in substance and luminosity. Gathering strength, it was as though I'd been caught in a glorious tractor beam of light from an unconditionally loving force inexorably drawing me forward into itself.

In this grace-filled inversion of polarities, I encountered the undifferentiated consciousness that predates our inception and to which we return upon dying, and which urges us forward toward awakening throughout the course of our lives. Seeing the truth that had all along been hidden in plain sight, I suddenly no longer experienced myself as having failed to retain my power or persona but rather as the harvest of archetypal and unconscious forces—and whatever choices I had been free to make culminating in this moment—*and that I was not in this alone.* As this shifting of the poles continued to unfold, I underwent the healing of my separated self. I became less fearful of dying, seeing death not as failure but as fulfillment of the arc of life. In its place, I intuited an inherent meaning to my life and newfound freedom. This was a tipping point that served as the mystical activation of my old soul. And now I had the answer to the many questions I'd asked over the course of the many stages through which I'd passed.

Viewing my life as a seeker from this side of the world of old souls, I finally understood the nature of the yearning that had determined the trajectory of my progression through the developmental arc. Previously, we have spoken of recovery. But recovery of what? Now we have the mystic's answer—of that for which we've yearned—reunification with the Divine. In the words of Evelyn Underhill, author of *The Mystic Way:* "The wistful eyes of life are set toward a vision that is also a Home—a Home from which news can reach us now and again . . . . It is a Becoming, yet a Being, a Growth yet a Consummation: the very substance of Eternity supporting and making actual the process of Time."

Even Scott-Maxwell, who complained noisily about her disappointment in humanity as well as her own shortcomings throughout much of her late-in-life journal shared her mystical apparition. Despite having endured two world wars, the Great Depression, the Viet Nam War, and the departure of her children to another continent, leaving her at 86 old, ill, and alone, she writes: "I am in that rare frame of mind when everything seems simple. When I have no doubt that the aim and solution of life is the acceptance of God . . . . I do not know what I seek, cannot know, but I am where the mystery is the certainty . . . . It can at moments feel as though we had it for our glory . . . a swelling clarity as though all was resolved."

You'll know that you have made it to the world of old souls when things that once caused you pain or compulsion no longer carry the power to devastate. Of course there are still gaps, tendrils from the well-worn furrows of the past in which you occasionally become entangled. But devoid of the pervasive sense of doomed wrongness, you find yourself enabled to disengage graciously and return to equanimity no matter the objective facts of your circumstance at any given time. The bar continues to be raised, and you will be called to rise again and again to meet the new challenges, some of which you will breeze through, some which will throw you for at least awhile. But even so, amends and forgiveness, even for new transgressions, come more quickly and easily, and you rarely fall into the pit of taking seriously the familiar but outgrown stories about your essential wrongness.

Ram Dass illustrates this new way of being in the world in a story about two waves in the ocean. One is tall. One is short. Both are rolling into the shore. The tall wave sees what's coming—waves crashing and dissolving back into the ocean—and starts to panic.

"We're going to die!"

The short wave is unconcerned. The tall wave shouts louder and louder, trying to convey the gravity of the situation. "Can't you see this is the end?"

But the short wave calmly responds: "What would you say if I told you that there are six words, that if you really understood and believed them, you would see that there's nothing to fear?"

"Yes! Please! Quickly! Tell me the six words!" pleads the tall wave.

The short wave replies: "You're not a wave, you're water."

Lured inexorably forward into merger with the Divine, one discovers a new reservoir of qualities to draw on. Patience; compassion for self, others, and the world; generosity; faith; unconditional love. And finally, however long or short your lifespan and the number of setbacks and breakthroughs along the way, there will at last be an arrival. None of the facts of your life need to change, you will still be you and, if anything, more so. But that which you have yearned for all your life will no longer elude you.

As Ralph Waldo Emerson wrote: "Certainly there is a right for you that needs no choice on your part. Place yourself in the middle of the stream of power and wisdom which flows into your life. Then, without effort, you are impelled to truth and perfect contentment." In Stage 9, the Big Reveal, you will have experienced a spiritual awakening. In Stage 10, your journey to culmination will accelerate exponentially as you live the rest of your days in the alternate universe of old souls and the unfolding fulfillment of life's promise.

The Land of Old Souls

Now we are beyond the narcissism of youth, above the survival struggles of young adulthood, beyond the grind of middle age, and prepared to look beyond ourselves into the very heartbeat of life . . . .We can do what our souls demand that fully human beings do. This is the moment for which we were born.

—Joan Chittister

FOR WEEKS AFTER MY BIG REVEAL, the conviction that something extraordinary had happened to me that day stayed with me unabated. After I left the cemetery, it was not that I never felt anxiety or anger or sadness. And grief. Lots of grief. But I could not deny it: there was something new happening. There were mornings when—just as, previously, I'd woken anxious—now there was joy. There were deep, unrecorded dreams that faded into awakening seamlessly, sunlit corners in which I found myself enjoying a cup of coffee with my husband without having had to work at recreating the meaning of life from scratch. Whatever the mood of the moment, I could see it all for what it is, what it always was. It was always only love lurking in the shadows. And not just love for the pretty objects, the tangible symbols of acceptance and success, but for the whole of it. Old age and, to be more accurate, the whole of life can be nothing we'd ever expected and more than we'd ever hoped for.

I would say I'd been transformed by the experience, but the truth is that "I" barely existed anymore. Often, the habit of myself to which I'd become accustomed was nowhere to be found. However, my routines remained largely the same. For instance, I'd previously committed to going out every afternoon, rain or shine, for exercise. But now as I walked through our quiet neighborhood, it was as if every tree pulsated with life informing me that they, not I, were the point. It wasn't long before each maple and birch in our yard had whispered to me its name. A worm crossing my path could bring me to a full stop, and I wasn't sure why that made me cry. Whereas I'd once pushed through my slowing pace as if my aging body were an obstacle, I determined to use the deficiencies of my energy and balky knees as the very vehicle that could strip away the last vestiges of my clinging to how things used to be. Day after day, through the changing seasons, I was carried to a place beyond expectations where, while the body was proving to be undependable, gratitude was not. This is a newfound ability, a gift of age: detaching from the fray of life, and my own ambition, to merge into a life that interacts with the world at a life-giving and age-appropriate pace, while rooted in the soul's natural habitat: appreciation of solitude. In this place of being, I grew deep and I grew whole. After years of having to channel the essence of my vitality to make something of myself, my spirit had, at last, found sanctuary.

In recording this, it sounds as if I were not just elevated but high. However, the experience was quite the opposite. I felt grounded and quiet in a way I was not accustomed to. As the days rolled along and I became more used to life as an old soul, it was as though something more meaningful than transcendence was pulling me into itself, something akin to a divine hug. What was the essence of this new experience of myself in relation to the world? It was that I was ordinary. And what's more, my ordinary self was sufficient. As Florida Scott-Maxwell put it so eloquently: "If in the end you have only yourself, it is enough."

Ordinary, I soon discovered, however, does not provide the same level of protection from life's shadows as the masks I'd so carefully constructed to give me cover. Of course, the headlines at night and phone calls by day continued to deliver a steady stream of bad news about the state of the world. Some of the bad news was deeply personal, reaching once again into the heart of our home just a few days ago. We were in a new season now, the wintry storms having given way over the course of my writing this book to a new spring: a full year after my walk in the cemetery. As I had every morning for the past 15 years, I'd woken early, listening for insistent paws scratching to go outside. But instead, there was utter silence. Sammy was curled up in his favorite doggy bed, but he was still. Too still. I called to Dan, and he rushed to my side to confirm what I feared. Overnight, our beloved Sammy—the last of our pack of dogs—had slipped away. Over the course of Covid, we had now lost all three of our dogs. The fact that Molly, the first to pass and at 10 the youngest, had terminal cancer, and that Lucky and Sammy—at 15 and 20—had outlived their breeds' life expectancy, and that we had spent the year lavishing each one with love did nothing to mitigate the grief of the loss. Old people often have old dogs and then lose them and so much more. It doesn't feel fair, and it doesn't alleviate the sorrow.

Once I had been given a glimpse of my inherent goodness, things could and did still go terribly wrong, but I was no longer able to take it personally. As it turns out, feeling bad is not the same as feeling bad about yourself. Living the *Serenity Prayer* in real time, after I'd done everything I could to make things right, all that was left for me to do was to accept the things I cannot change. When I removed the unspoken dread that it would always have been up to me to do something more, better, or different to get things to turn out if only I'd tried hard enough, what remained was unvarnished reality. And, through the grace of God, there was growing compassion for self, others, and the human condition. Permeating it all: love.

Reality includes allowing yourself to have authentic feelings. In fact, rather than the placidity some gerontologists prefer for their sedated patients, the depth of emotion that is unleashed in the making of an old soul is likely to take you by surprise. Parker J. Palmer writes in *On the Brink of Everything: Grace, Gravity and Getting Old*: "Reality may be hard, but it's a safer place to live than in our illusions, which will always fail us, and at no point is that more true than in old age . . . .Coming to terms with the soul-truth of who I am—with my complex and confusing mix of darkness and light—has required my ego to shrivel up. Nothing shrivels a person better than age. That's what all those wrinkles are about."

I am reminded here of my favorite story about the Dalai Lama told by Olivia Ames Hoblitzelle, author of *Aging with Wisdom*. At one of his annual three-day retreats in New York City, the Dalai Lama "explained that when we open to the experience of interconnectedness with the world, our sense of individuality softens and the heart opens with compassion toward all beings. This compassion has radiance about it, he added. Suddenly he paused, interrupting his own train of thought. 'But that's not the way things are,' he shared. 'We are just people groping in the dark,' and he put his head down and began to weep openly. After a few moments, he sat up, blew his nose, and continued where he'd left off."

If we want to be more fully alive, we must eschew simplistic spiritual and philosophical formulations that limit us to conventional understandings of happiness, including the stereotypes of what it means to age gracefully. Burst through to the world of old souls, and you will find what you've been searching for from the beginning without knowing it: an expanded awareness that leaves nothing out. Yes, you didn't get everything you wanted as a child, and you will not as an adult; yes, it is scary to admit that some things are beyond your control—take the future, for instance—and, no matter how much therapy and meditation you do, you will still never be able to get everything to turn out the way you hope. You'll lose those you care for. You'll be misunderstood. You'll be alone—sometimes. And you will die—for sure. Growing up spiritually doesn't mean you no longer have your original wound, the ramifications of what remains of your unintended consequences and all the stories and emotions that you bundled up with it. It doesn't mean you don't ever again experience old, familiar places of sadness, anger, jealousy, fear, and despair. And when in the moment of reactivity you forget everything you've ever learned, it won't be the last time you will ever turn against yourself. But when you do, you will now know yourself well enough to trust that, while you may not be able to avoid visiting these lost places from time to time, you do not need to take up permanent residence.

Here's how Yogi Sri Aurobindo puts it, "You get up, you take a step, you fall on your face, you get up, you look sheepishly at God, you brush yourself off, you take another step, you fall on your face, you get up, you look sheepishly at God, you brush yourself off, you take another step . . . ." Having come this far, you now have the capacity to witness the cycle of reactivity with a heightened degree of consciousness, to see the part you are playing, and to use the tools of Conscious Aging to help you break out of it. This includes remembering that there are times when all you can do is give up trying and throw yourself on God's mercy, begging for help.

For years, when our generation spoke of fulfilling the human potential, we pointed ourselves in the direction of only the brighter hues of the spectrum: happiness, joy, peace, and the like. What we didn't understand is that, in doing so, we had consigned ourselves to what was, in reality, a narrow slice on the greater band of possibilities. To aspire to becoming whole, we must avail ourselves of the shadow as well as the light: bittersweet sorrow, righteous anger, heart-rending grief, even abject humiliation. These, too, are part of the human potential. You only became fully conscious of the voice in your mind that had been quietly, persistently judging your every move, defining the contours of your persona, limiting you in ways you did not previously understand, by its absence. When you cross into the world of old souls, you will discover that, in the true fulfillment of your human potential, you can be at once anything, everything, and nothing. But still don't take even your *nobodyness* too seriously.

After chanting Buddha's name for years, an old woman suddenly felt "all the falsehoods of her life drop away and she is completely and utterly awake," Geri Larkin writes in "The Secret of Abiding Joy," an article in *Spirituality and Health*.

"Thrilled, the old woman rushes to see the great Zen Master Hakuin, telling him that her whole body is filled with Buddha and that all of the mountains and rivers, forests and fields are shining with great enlightenment. He looks at her: 'Oh really?' he says. 'And is this great light also shining up your butt?' Even though the old woman is tiny, she pushes him over, shouting, 'Well, I can see you still have work to do yourself, old man!' They laugh themselves silly and are so happy that they dance and dance and dance—awakeness meeting awakeness."

Sometimes, all we can do is laugh ourselves silly. Reb Zalman Schachter-Shalomi shares that there were plenty of times he turned inward seeking guidance from his inner rebbi, only to be greeted instead by his inner nebbish. Likewise, James Hillman, author of *The Force of Character and the Lasting Life*, doesn't flinch when he looks into the shadows of his own quirky character eye-to-eye. And what's more, as a Jungian psychologist, he can see more clearly in the dark.

It didn't take long for me to locate my own incorrigible brand of personality traits on his list of human foibles, including bouts of muddled agitation and deluded bravado. But Hillman does not judge any of this. In fact, he relishes all of our imperfection as the embodiment of unavoidable archetypes necessary to the whole. He writes: "Aging brings out all sorts of contradictions in human nature. All the complexes composing personality leap out of the basket. You become an unpredictable hydra—smiling, snapping, happy, grouchy, grumpy—all seven dwarfs."

According to Hillman we can do what we can to cultivate more desirable habits, but we will never succeed at achieving the oversimplified ideal our culture thinks of as being of *good character*. Rather, we can cultivate an appreciation for *force of character*. Some of what he means by this "is the persistence of the incorrigible anomalies, those traits you can't fix, can't hide, and can't accept . . . . Resolutions, therapy, conversion, the heart's contrition in old age—nothing prevails against them, not even prayer. We are left realizing that character is indeed a force that cannot succumb to willpower . . . . [Rather,] character forces me to encounter each event in my peculiar style. It forces me to differ. I walk through life oddly. No one else walks as I do, and this is my courage, my dignity, my integrity, my morality, and my ruin."

So what are we left with in this romp toward a final reckoning? In an understanding that disavows fixing, what you think of as unwanted traits do not magically transform into serenity. When you embrace your anger, you are still angry. Embrace your naivety, you are still naive. But as I noted earlier, we are not only our least desirable traits. One assumes that there are things we like—even love—about ourselves and the world, as well. But better yet, in Stage 10 it is time to stop making the fool-hearted attempt to define yourself as good or bad, right or wrong, or according to your likes and dislikes. You are not only the favored child, the good or bad mother, the endlessly giving spouse, or the selfish friend. The encounter with your authenticity in the world of old souls jettisons the old masks to reveal a unique eccentricity that has less to do with striving for moral perfection and more to do with appreciating yourself as a force of nature.

I can assure you, this letting go of the retelling of the narrative of your original wounds and accepting that there are things about yourself that you will never overcome feels counter-intuitive at first. But there comes a time when the sheer magnitude of who you really are and what you have made of your life can no longer be circumscribed by the size of your old story, and at last the container breaks wide open. One of the greatest gifts of growing older is that we're not nearly as fascinated with our original wounds as we used to be. It's not that we don't fall into the pit of feeling we weren't loved the way we deserved, the fear that we may be abandoned or that we're inherently not good enough. But by now we've run these storylines so many times, they've become boring even to ourselves. Somewhere along the way, if we are lucky, we come to realize that, while the process of spiritual growth does indeed entail opening old wounds, this is just the beginning. After we have sucked the denial-busting juice of productivity out of them here's the kicker: we are meant to get on with it. At this point, the conversation between old souls changes dramatically. Yes, the hits keep coming, but no longer does every transgression need be assigned a villain; nor does every disappointment trigger the need to try harder to reassert control. In fact, the things that others do to us, the things that happen to us, no longer inspire, at worst, never-ending accusations and victimhood— at best, endless self-examination and self-mortification. And at last, there comes a time when the harrowing nature of the work is done. Parker J. Palmer writes: "I have plowed my life this way. Turned over a whole history. Looking for the roots of what went wrong. Until my face is ravaged, furrowed, scarred. Enough. The job is done. Whatever's been uprooted, let it be. Seedbed for the growing that's to come . . . ."

And that's when things get really interesting. Singh wrote toward the end of her life: "Eventually, as we continue to engage these last years for spiritual practice, we come to see that every moment, every interaction, every circumstance arises from the ground of being . . . . All of it—the smiles, the wind, the lovemaking, the hearing aid, the knee replacement, the pink slip, the warmth of the sun, the cancer, the scent of lilacs, the funeral, the slip in the snow. It's all part of the path."

Yes, there are losses. But there are also gains. Each moment of every one of our increasingly precious days, we are at a crossroads. We have spoken repeatedly of the large degree of unconsciousness over which we have no control. But we have also been working hard and long through the arc of life, all of it in service of wresting more and more consciousness out of the whole. We wouldn't have made it this far if we hadn't succeeded. Our capacity to tell the truth, to see clearly, to discern the best possibilities given our circumstances has grown exponentially. We can use our expanded awareness coupled with free will to respond more efficiently than ever to the Divine's call to make the best, most life-giving choice in any given moment. Will you? This is no small question, as letting go of everything that brought you this far makes you vulnerable in ways you had never anticipated—did not know you had in you. Scott-Maxwell describes this way of being, and the price you pay for it in courage, pain, and humility. "The ordeal of being true to your own inner way must stand high on the list of ordeals. It is like being in the power of someone you cannot reach, know, or move, but who never lets you go . . . . It is not easy to be sure that being yourself is worth the trouble, but we do know it is our sacred duty."

I am many things today that I wasn't months ago, let alone years. I am less liable to be bullied, more self-nurturing, less worried about what others think and how things look, and generally more apt to bound out the front door eager to experience whatever new adventures may come my way. I understand more about what it means to love and be loved, and how to tender compassion without strings attached. And yet, on any given day, I may also be devastated at some point, ecstatic at another, and for the rest I am often just doing— well, whatever. At my best, I suppose I am in that state for which I have so mightily striven over the years: simply living in the present moment. But since the whole point of Ram Dass's notion of "being here now" is to be devoid of commentary or concern, there is quite simply no witness to render judgment—happy or sad.

The making of an old soul asks almost more of you than you can bear. For the remainder of your journey, however easy or difficult, all you can do is hold yourself tightly with as much compassion as you can muster for yourself, the world, and the human condition. Whatever comes your way, you let yourself feel whatever arises with no need to understand it or to do something about it. There must be something to it that Singh, Scott-Maxwell, Hillman, Ram Dass and so many others who have touched this place of utter surrender ask us variations of the question: *What is it that can't be lost to you?* To which I can, at last, reply: "Let's take a walk, hold hands, cry together, laugh, too, and if we have to say anything at all, let it be *Amen*."

Fulfilling Life's Promise

A T LAST WE ARRIVE at the peak of the progression through life stages, already collecting on the fulfillment of life's promise that we have sought for so long. With all the emphasis on accepting our powerlessness and the lack of guarantees, how could I have known all along that this was a promise that would be kept? For the answer, we must dive deep into our own personal as well as communal experiences tending to those at the end of life. Many who have worked in hospice care observe a spiritual quickening in the final stretch. Singh, who spent many hours at the side of people on their death beds, writes: "One of the most meaningful things that often happens as a terminally ill person dies can best be described as 'the opening of the heart' . . . . The opening of the heart is a radical release of all that doesn't matter—of all that has always kept our heart closed. When our heart opens, we lose nothing. Nothing that can be lost is real. As we die and the heart opens, we are no longer, in Nisargadatta's piercing phrase, 'burdened with a person.'"

In Singh's words, I recognized both what I'd experienced holding my mother's hand over the course of her last breath, as well as the life review that passed before my own eyes that day in the cemetery. From Singh and others, I have learned that even those who have gone kicking and screaming out of life can experience this sudden merger with the Divine. This is what happened to Ivan Ilyich in Leo Tolstoy's enduring classic *The Death of Ivan Ilyich*. The novel relates the story of the illness and agonizing death of a mediocre judge who hid all his life behind a mask of grandiosity and an inflated sense of entitlement. With a mix of understated horror and fascination, Tolstoy details Ivan's weak defenses against the onset of terminal illness, the hard-earned lack of sincere care from those around him, and the unwitting contributions he made to both their suffering and his own. But in the span of his last breath, even Ivan experiences redemption. As his masks crumble, Ivan sees all that he'd missed in life, all that truly matters, and asks to be forgiven. Tolstoy writes: "Suddenly it became clear to him that what had been oppressing him and would not leave him suddenly was vanishing all at once . . . . 'And death? Where is it?' He searched for his accustomed fear of death and could not find it. Where was death? What death? There was no fear because there was no death. Instead of death there was light. 'So that's it!' he exclaimed. 'What bliss!' All this happened in a single moment, but the significance of the moment was lasting."

This opportunity for hope Tolstoy gives the reader comes on the last page of his book, and thank God that it comes at all. But what if the awakening you have so long sought could come well before your final page, and you could enjoy the joy and freedom of merger with the Divine with time to spare? "For the dying, this committed practice of bringing attention to the present moment occurs on the hospital bed. It is choiceless," writes Singh. However, for those of us who still have breath remaining, there is a choice that must be made. Singh continues,

"We need to decide if we really want to live and die smaller and more impoverished than we need to be. If we have any desire to ripen into spiritual maturity—into the abiding experience of the sacred, of all that iies beyond this small self—now is the time."

Both Singh and Tolstoy share a vision of hope that holds the potential to transcend our worst fears about the end of life and what comes after. Tolstoy writes: "Try to live with the part of your soul which understands eternity, which is not afraid of death. And that part of your soul is love." This is not to say that the potential for suffering isn't real—not to be romanticized or minimized in any way. Pain, grief, loss, and the unfinished business of life must be acknowledged and respected. In the words of poet Jennifer Welwood:

My friends, let's grow up.
Let's stop pretending we don't know the deal here . . .
Let's grieve our losses fully, like ripe human beings,
But please, let's not be so shocked by them.

Having come this far through the arc of life to Stage 11 doesn't mean there isn't still a long way for us to go, especially with old age continually presenting new challenges. We have applied ourselves for more years than we can count to expanding our consciousness in hopes of heading off the unnecessary suffering of an Ivan Ilyich, or perhaps someone you've attended to closer to home. But even the most spiritual amongst us have a hard time giving up the last-minute negotiation for safe passage. In fact, Ram Dass, who sat at the death bed of many committed spiritual practitioners, reports that what was causing the greatest suffering had less to do with physical pain and more to do with the mistaken notion that there is a "right" way to die. Under the spell of this mistaken notion, one is liable to fear that if one were experiencing anything other than serenity, acceptance, and bliss, one was failing this last spiritual challenge. In a previous life stage, you had to accept rather than reject all the seven dwarfs that comprise the essence of your unique walk through life. So are you now called upon to cease bracing yourself against the possibility that, in your final hour, you may cry out at the injustice of what is being asked of you. The very real potential for suffering at the end is hard enough. You don't need to add to it by turning against yourself, feeling that if only you were worthy enough, you could rise above it. Just as the entry from merger to life through birth is accompanied by an initiatory trial, so may the return from life to merger through death require a culminating struggle. Reality is rarely easy. But what's the alternative? Palmer reminds us of the exchange between the 19th-century transcendentalist Margaret Fuller and the writer Thomas Carlyle: "'I accept the universe,' proclaimed Fuller. 'Gad! She'd better,' replied Carlyle."

The reality is that we enter the world crying out in pain, and so we may depart. The difference is that, in the latter case, the lifetime of separation is behind us and, regardless of how awe-some or awe-ful, there will at last be an arrival. Rabbi Alan Lew, in *This Is Real and You Are Completely Unprepared*, puts it like this. "There is the overwhelmingly senseless gratitude we feel when we are finally fully awake. And it makes no difference what we awaken to, whether it is to pain or to pleasure, to life or to death; it is all of a piece, all the ground of a deep joy when fully inhabited, when wholly attended to." Lew speaks of merger with the Divine if not at the end of our lives, in the end of days. But for those of us who hope to experience this sooner, there's more good news. You, after all, are reading this now, so there's still time. Be it by mystical revelation or the methodical accumulation of experience, your progression through the arc of life has brought you this far to a place of choice. As poet Mary Oliver asks of us all: "Tell me, what is it you plan to do with your one wild and precious life?" Serenity, as it is commonly understood, is not the only answer. Yes, I love walking in nature and cherish quiet time curled up with a volume of Thomas Merton before a blazing fireplace. But I have also learned to let loose in ways I'd never anticipated. Here's an example from Isaac Bashevis Singer's novel *The Family Moskat* that makes me smile every time I read it:

> I'm getting as old as Methuselah; I climb a single flight of stairs and my heart begins to pound like a thief's with the police after him . . . . I went to Dr. Mintz.
>
> "Don't get yourself excited," he says. "Bad for your belly-button."
>
> "Aha," I tell him, "a fine trick if you can do it. Suppose you try, doctor," I tell him.
>
> He imagines that all I have to do is stretch out on the sofa, close my peepers, and everything is settled.
>
> "That's not my way, professor. I have to roar like a lion. Do you hear me, professor? If I wasn't ashamed, I would let out such a roaring that Warsaw would collapse.'

Today, you, too, might want to roar like a lion. Another day, you may prefer to purr. Hopefully there's time for laughter, for getting together with friends, for traveling to see the kids, for doing good deeds, or for simply goofing off. I'm not saying it is easy to shake off a lifetime of conditioning. We are meant in our old age to assess our lives, weighing and balancing our assets in a final reckoning. But by whose criteria? By whose values shall we deem our lives to have been a success or a failure? Late in life, your husband left you for a younger woman. Your godson is in rehab. The last of your books went out of print. All your life, you have defended yourself against the utter failure your original wound warned you about. How much of your life have you allowed to slip by not only worrying about the unwanted things that have, are, or could be happening to you, but standing accused by others and, even worse, by yourself regarding your inherent unworthiness?

When you have transited through the developmental stages described in this book and have taken up residence, at last, in the world of old souls, life will make good on its promise to you. I'm speaking here from experience, having carried the burden of my original wound—separation from the Divine— through more years than I care to admit. The biggest reveal of all that came to me that day in the cemetery was that, devoid of the voice of judgment whispering to me of things amiss, my heart had not shattered but rather, miraculously, had expanded to embrace it all. "Nothing less than bearing it all will do, for it is the creation of a change of consciousness," writes Scott-Maxwell. "Nothing less and no words are needed. It is the mystery that is done to us; as though love and pain and emergence are all intensified energy by which one is fired, ordered and perhaps annealed. The purpose of life may be to clarify our essence, and everything else is the rich, dull, hard, absorbing chaos that allows the central transmutation."

The revision of the arc of life that was revealed to me in the cemetery makes it explicit that, for seekers, the inclination to be an old soul initiates with the first life stage. The trajectory and velocity of our passage through the remaining 10 stages will be largely determined by a genetic inheritance that includes passion, discontent, and insatiable curiosity—a particular persistence all seekers share that borders on stubbornness. From childhood on, you had to make difficult choices—not just once, but over and over again. As you grew through life stages, you had to be willing to lean into rather than deny discomforting truths about yourself and the world. When you crossed the portal into the world of old souls, you came to hone your sensibilities to attune to the joy inherent in creation. And here, transiting through Stage 11 at the peak of adult development, you are taking dangerous risks to be true to yourself. You are submitting to the urge to fall to your knees in wonder. And you are allowing yourself to be loved unconditionally, coming to trust that you are deserving for no particular reason. And when you forget, as you will, you will learn from your mistakes and do better, one choice at a time.

There is nothing about this that is quiescent. Nobodyness, like white, is not the absence of color but made up of the entire range of possibilities. You may one day find yourself staring out the window, doing nothing more than appreciating the play of light and shadow on the leaves. On another, you may find yourself with a megaphone to your lips, waking up the previously dormant heart of an activist, a prophet, a leader, a creator. And if you have already been these things, this time "doing" will be inspired, not driven. You won't be spending time securing your legacy, worrying about what it all amounted to. You will simply be living life to the full in all its intended intensity.

In Stage 11, *Fulfilling Life's Promise*, you come to view the whole of your life through new eyes, appreciating all the beauty and love that were there all along not only despite but because of the circumstances and attributes to which you were born and the choices you made along the way. Like switching the light from off to on in the favorite room of your home, nothing will apparently change nor needs to. When you arrive at Stage 11, all the furniture will be just as you left it.

In my favorite room, the hand-made throw knitted long ago by my mother in her final months is still draped casually over the arm of my favorite chair. Photos of children and grandchildren at various ages are illuminated under spotlights on every counter and wall. Decades of trinkets and gifts given in celebration of one milestone or another are scattered about. A bookshelf of all the books I've loved to read and to write. Where there was once the vague sense that, despite knowing how much there was to be grateful for something was amiss, there is now only the bittersweet acceptance that all is exactly as it was meant to be, and that it's enough. My heart has not been broken by life. It has grown large enough to embrace even the overstuffed chair in front of the fire where my beloved husband now sits, his lap where one or another of our dogs used to curl up now empty, but his heart is full. So much love. So many tears. Here, at this moment of culmination, we can finally reap the harvest of the years we've invested in bringing as much consciousness as we can bear to become fierce with age. Here, in the world of old souls, we shall be as the Seraphim in Chassidic Midrash, angels in attendance to God, whose only job is to recite "Holy, Holy, Holy" three times. The thing is, the heat of their passion is so fervent, they can only get partway through the first holy before burning up.

What the world needs now, more than ever, is more love and more consciousness—of large things previously denied and small things previously unnoticed. We can hold onto our old, habitual ways of seeing ourselves and the world, or allow both the pathos and the beauty of life, in all its vulnerability, to break us open. It is as Robert Jingen Gunn in *Journey to Emptiness* writes: We can shut down in the face of crisis and tragedy, or we can let it take us "to the exact edge of life and death . . . . There we are forced to make a choice about how to live: whether to follow vitality with its attendant risks, struggles and promise, or whether to succumb to the death within life of unconsciousness."

When the portal to the secret world of old souls opened for me, I was increasingly motivated by no-strings-attached love and less and less by the will to power over others or circumstances regardless of how noble my intentions. I discovered that I could be both patient and passionate, kind and fierce. I could even discover that I had the capacity to suffer and witness pain caused by circumstances beyond my control without turning against myself. Speaking to the existential nature of the choice that is ours to make, James Hollis writes: "Those who have gone through that transformation have been to Hell and need not fear it anymore; they know that life will bring further tests but will not allow them to settle back into the old, familiar place. From that point onward, they live with a deeper integrity and are less and less defined by the old fears or the many hysterias found all around them. The price and the often grave consequences are compensated through a more profound experience of meaning, whether or not it is ratified by one's tribe."

Since the day of my walk in the cemetery, the irrepressible core that is the essence of who I am at heart is once again bursting through. I am glimpsing what it is to go all in on who I really am, but finding it more durable this time than I had previously understood. I am not being careful. I am saying words that should have been spoken years ago; facing old wounds and harsh realities with courage rather than fear; quitting whatever it is I've outgrown. All the while, I'm leaving lots of room for improvisation, proving nothing to nobody. I

am, in short, like my old friend Shelly, growing not just old—
but wild.

Despite setbacks, stall-outs and misunderstandings, you,
too, have prayed hard and long to God to power the oars of
your intention as you navigated through the sometimes sibilant,
other times rough seas of instinct, habit, and unintended
consequences to the once distant shore inhabited by the band
of hardy old souls that you have always been destined to join.
These are the essential ingredients that go into the making of an
old soul and the means by which you finally make good on the
fulfillment of life's promise, one rise and one fall at a time. And
yet, even having access to every secret conscribed by the arc of
life, every report passed down by the fierce ones who walked
this path before, it will still not be up to you to bring it about.
No matter how much you have committed to the journey
through life, how determined, how persistent, how brave, how
forgiving, how compassionate, how surrendered, how patient
you are, there always was and always will be *something more.*

Acknowledgments

The Making of an Old Soul caps my career of over 30 books, each one bearing an acknowledgement of my debt of gratitude. As I review the succession of agents and publishers, friends and supporters, it is as though I've been lovingly passed hand-to-hand through my life to the present moment. While some of the cast of characters have changed, there are regulars who made their appearances early on and have become the warp and weave of my life and career. And so it is to all of you I give my deepest thanks.

To my current publisher, former agent, and lifelong friend, Linda Roghaar, and the inspired team at White River Press: Your love of books and support of my work have sustained me through the many ups and downs of the writing life. And to Susan Rios, artist and dear friend, for providing the glorious cover art for my two favorite books. Thank you.

To the Vanderbilt Divinity School community for opening my mind and my heart as a student and for allowing me the privilege of giving back as a member of the Board of Visitors.

To the tribe of old souls, fellow authors, collaborators, and friends, who make life in the alternate universe of aging a joy. To

John C. Robinson, who suggested that my mystical experience be turned into a book; and to Robert L. Weber, Brent Green, H. Rick Moody, Jerome Kerner, Rosemary Cox, and the Sage-ing Book Club.

To my Nashville network of soulmates including Jill, Judith, Pat, Adele, Deb, and a special thanks to Marika Schoenberger and to the SAN Zoomers who sustained me through the darkest days of lockdown.

To my extended family, my cousins on the Matzkin, Nemeroff, and Mayers branches of the family tree, with special thanks to my soul sisters Fonda, Leean, and Sue.

To my pack of angels, Lucky, Molly and Sammy. Thank you for being our dogs.

And above all, to my family: my beloved Dan; Grant and Ginny and grandsons Mason and Dylan; Jody and Diego and our newest granddoggy, Captain Nemo, "Capi."

My gratitude to all of you is fierce indeed!

Sources of Quotes
and Inspiration

Al-Anon Family Group Head, Inc. *One Day at a Time in Al-Anon*. Virginia Beach: Al-Anon Family Group Headquarters Inc., 2000.

Aurobindo, Sri. Quoted by Ram Dass: www.ramdass.org/turning-ego -heart, 2021.

Chittister, Joan. *The Gift of Years: Growing Older Gracefully*. New York: BlueBridge, 2008.

Chodron, Pema. *Start Where You Are: A Guide to Compassionate Living*. Boston: Shambhala Publishing, 1994.

Cobb, John B. Jr. and David Ray Griffin. *Process Theology: An Introductory Exposition*. Philadelphia: The Westminster Press, 1976.

Davidson, Sara. *The December Project: An Extraordinary Rabbi and a Skeptical Seeker Confront Life's Greatest Mystery*. New York: HarperOne, 2014.

Emerson, Ralph Waldo. *Emerson's Essays: The First and Second Series Complete*. Paris: Adansonia Publishing, 2018.

Erikson, Erik H. *The Life Cycle Completed: A Review*. New York: W.W. Norton & Company, 1982.

Erikson, Joan M. *Wisdom and the Senses: The Way of Creativity.* New York: W.W. Norton & Company, 1988.

Fowler, J.W. *Stages of Faith: The Psychology of Human Development and the Quest for Meaning.* New York: Harper & Row, 1981.

Green, Brent, et al. *1969: Are You Still Listening?* Denver, Colo.: Brent Green & Assoc., 2019.

————.*Questions of the Spirit: The Quest for Understanding at a Time of Loss.* Denver, Colo.: Brent Green & Assoc., 2017.

Gunn, Robert Jingen. *Journey to Emptiness: Dogen, Merton, Jung and the Quest for Transformation.* Mahwah, N.J.: Paulist Press, 2000.

Hillman, James. *The Force of Character and the Lasting Life.* New York: Random House, 1999.

Hoblitzelle, Olivia James. *Aging with Wisdom: Reflections, Stories & Teachings.* Rhinebeck, N.Y.: Monkfish Publishing, 2017.

Hollis, James. *Finding Meaning in the Second Half of Life: How to Finally, Really Grow Up.* New York: Gotham Books, 2005.

————. Living *Between Worlds: Finding Personal Resilience in Changing Times.* Boulder, Colo.: Sounds True, 2020.

James, William. *The Varieties of Religious Experience: A Study in Human Nature.* New York:Collier Books, 1961.

Jung, C .G. *Memories, Dreams, Reflections.* New York: Vintage Books, 1989.

Kuner, Susan, and Carol Orsborn, Linda Quigley, Karen Stroup. *Speak the Language of Healing: Living with Breast Cancer without Going to War.* Foreword by Jean Shinoda Bolen, M.D. Berkeley, Calif.: Conari Press, 1997.

Lew, Alan. *This Is Real and You Are Completely Unprepared.* Boston: Little, Brown, 2003.

Levinson, Daniel, with Charlotte Darrow, Edward Klein, Maria Levinson, and Braxton McKee. *The Seasons of a Man's Life.* New York: Alfred A. Knopf, 1978.

Mansfield, Katherine *The Katherine Mansfield Notebooks, Complete Edition*. Minneapolis: University of Minnesota Press, 2002.

May, Rollo. *The Courage to Create*. New York: W.W. Norton & Company, 1975.

Merton, Thomas. *No Man Is an Island*. New York: Image/Doubleday, 1955.

———. *The Seven Storey Mountain*. New York: Harcourt, 1948.

———. *The Silent Life*. New York: Dell, 1957, and New York: Farrar, Strauss and Giroux, 1999.

Metzger, Bruce M., and Roland E. Murphy. *The New Oxford Annotated Bible*. New York: Oxford University Press, 1991.

Moody, Harry R., and David Carroll. *The Five Stages of the Soul*. New York: Anchor Books, 1997.

Niebuhr, Reinhold. Quoted in *Grapevine: The International Journal of Alcoholics Anonymous*, January 1950, 6–7.

Nouwen, Henri J. M., and Walter J. Gaffney. *Aging: The Fulfillment of Life*. New York: Image Books, 1976.

Oliver, Mary. "The Summer Day." *House of Light*. Boston: Beacon Press, 1990.

Orsborn, Carol. *Angelica's Last Breath*. Nashville, Tenn.: Fierce with Age Press, 2018.

———. *The Art of Resilience: 100 Paths to Wisdom and Strength in an Uncertain World*. New York: Random House, 1997.

———. *Enough Is Enough: Exploding the Myth of Having It All*. New York: Putnam, 1986.

———. *How Would Confucius Ask for a Raise: One Hundred Enlightened Solutions for Tough Business Problems*. New York: Avon, 1994.

———. *Fierce with Age: Chasing God and Squirrels in Brooklyn*. Nashville, Tenn.: Turner Publishing, 2013.

———. *Nothing Left Unsaid: Words to Help You and Your Loved Ones through the Hardest Time*. Berkeley, Calif.: Conari Press, 2001.

————. *Older, Wiser, Fiercer: The Wisdom Collection.* Nashville, Tenn.: Fierce with Age Press, 2020.

————. *Solved by Sunset: The Self-Guided Intuitive Decision-Making Retreat.* New York: Random House, 1996, and New York: Crown, 1997.

Otto, Rudolf. *The Idea of the Holy.* London: Oxford University Press, 1958.

Palmer, Parker J. *On the Brink of Everything: Grace, Gravity & Getting Old.* Oakland, Calif.: Berrett-Koehler Publishers Inc., 2018.

Perry, Glynys. *Coping with Crisis.* New York: Routledge, Chapman and Hall, 1990.

Piaget, Jean. *The Construction of Reality in the Child.* (M. Cook, trans.). New York: Basic Books, 1954.

Ram Dass. *Still Here: Embracing Aging, Changing, and Dying.* New York: Penguin Books, 2000.

Robinson, John C. *The Three Secrets of Aging: A Radical Guide.* Winchester, UK: O-Books, 2012.

————. *The Divine Human: The Final Transformation of Sacred Aging,* Winchester, England: O-Books, 2016.

Rohr, Richard. *Falling Upward: A Spirituality for the Two Halves of Life.* San Francisco: Jossey-Bass, 2011.

Roof, Wade Clark. *A Generation of Seekers: The Spiritual Journeys of the Baby Boom Generation.* San Francisco: HarperSanFrancisco, 1994.

Schachter-Shalomi, Zalman. *From Age-ing to Sage-ing: A Profound New Vision of Growing Older.* New York: Oxford University Press, 1997.

Scott-Maxwell, Florida. *The Measure of My Days: One Woman's Vivid, Enduring Celebration of Life and Aging.* New York: Penguin Books, 1968.

Shapiro, Rami. *Recovery: The Sacred Art.* Nashville: SkyLight Paths Publishing, 2009.

Sheehy, Gail. *New Passages: Mapping Your Life Across Time.* New York: Random House, 1995.

Singer, Isaac Bashevitz. *The Family Moskat*. New York: Farrar, Straus and Giroux, 2007.

Singh, Katherine Dowling. *The Grace in Aging: Awaken as You Grow Older*. Somerville, Mass.: Wisdom Publications, 2014.

Thibault, Jane Marie. "Aging as a Natural Monastery." *Aging & Spirituality: Newsletter of the American Society on Aging's Forum on Religion, Spirituality and Aging*. San Francisco, 1996.

———. *A Deepening Love Affair: The Gift of God in Later Life*. Nashville, Tenn.: Upper Room Books, 1993.

Thibault, Jane Marie, and Richard L. Morgan. *Pilgrimage into the Last Third of Life: 7 Gateways to Spiritual Growth*. Nashville, Tenn.: Upper Room Books, 2012.

Tolstoy, Leo. *The Death of Ivan Ilyich*. New York: Bantam Classic, 2004.

Underhill, Evelyn. *The Mystic Way*. London: Forgotten Books, 2013.

———. *Practical Mysticism: A Little Book for Normal People*. New York: Dutton, 1943.

Weber, Robert L. and Carol Orsborn. *The Spirituality of Age: A Seeker's Guide to Growing Older*. Rochester, Vt.: Inner Traditions, 2015.

Welwood, Jennifer. *The Dakiini Speaks*. jenniferwelwood.com/poetry /the-dakini-speaks, 2021.

Wilhelm, Hellmut, ed. (Cary F. Baynes, trans.) *The I Ching*. Princeton, NJ: Princeton University Press, 1967.

Yalom, Irvin D. *Staring at the Sun: Overcoming the Dread of Death*. San Francisco: Jossey-Bass, 2008.

About the Author

Carol Orsborn, Ph.D. is a recognized thought leader in the field of Conscious Aging and author of 30 books translated into 15 languages, including her most recent book, *Older, Wiser, Fiercer: The Wisdom Collection*. Her award-winning book, *The Spirituality of Age: A Seeker's Guide to Growing Older*, coauthored with Harvard psychologist Robert Weber, Ph.D., won Gold in the 2015 Nautilus Book Awards in the category of Aging Consciously. Orsborn is chief archivist at *Fierce with Age, the Digest of Boomer Wisdom, Inspiration and Spirituality* housed at CarolOrsborn.com. She also founded and co-leads the Sage-ing International Book Club. For the past 40 years, Orsborn has been a compelling voice of her generation, interviewed on *Oprah, The Today Show, CBS Morning News*, and *The Shift Network*, and in the *New York Times*, and many others. She has spoken frequently at the American Society of Aging, Sage-ing International, the Shift Network and the Positive Aging Conference.

Dr. Orsborn, a Phi Beta Kappa graduate of the University of California, Berkeley, received her Master of Theological Studies from Vanderbilt Divinity School and Doctorate in History and Critical Theory of Religion from Vanderbilt University specializing in the areas of adult and spiritual development, and ritual studies. She serves on the community leadership Board of Visitors of Vanderbilt Divinity School. She is a certified spiritual counselor with postgraduate work in Spiritual Counseling at the New Seminary in Manhattan, Stillpoint, and the Spirituality Center at Mount St. Mary's College. A former top marketer, helping brands like Ford, Humana, and Prudential build relationships with the boomer generation, she is now committed to both living and expanding awareness of aging as a spiritual path. Dr. Orsborn lives on the banks of the Cumberland River in Madison, Tennessee with her husband of over fifty years, Dan.

Invitation to Stay Connected

Carol Orsborn's Conscious Aging and Sage-ing International book clubs welcome you to join the conversation on the classics of the spirituality and aging genre. Meeting via Zoom and online, the virtual club, including a reader's guide for The Making of an Old Soul, *can be accessed at the Book Club tab at CarolOrsborn.com*

The website also features Carol's blog, the Fierce with Age Archives, a self-guided retreat, and updates on related offerings.

CPSIA information can be obtained
at www.ICGtesting.com
Printed in the USA
LVHW031555251021
701446LV00002B/329